THE SPELL OF SIX DRAGONS

James True

To my family.

Table of Contents

CHAPTER ONE

Jimmy

The Sound of a Voice

Words like smoke in a lazy room
Sheets of gray and silver gloom
Into my ears please ring your tune
The sound of a voice
An echo in the halls of my head
Lips send spaces silence fed
Hungry hollow ears are led
The sound of a voice
So much happens in her face
In these arms I rest my case
If I am guilty please erase
The sound of a voice

Those jog offs in the coveralls lost my Big Wheel. I should have slept with that thing till it got up here to the mountains. My head would have found comfort on that hollow plastic saddle with the smell of dyed petroleum melting in the sunlight. My three-wheeled Hi-Yo silver with tassels was gone. Those jog offs in the yellow moving truck lost you. What's a boy to do without his horse? I collapsed into a crumbled mass of stranded goo in the driveway. I was melting in the sun like spat gum. My horse was still out there, wondering what had happened to his ranger. I pictured her in my former driveway, the sun was setting and she still thinks I'm coming home. There were attempts to console me with the offer of a newer contraption called a Green Machine. The other kids had one but it felt too much like a form of betrayal. I developed a flavor for walking. I wasn't ready for another relationship.

A plan was concocted, reviewed and rubber-stamped by all parties. My brother would light, and I would toss. It was a firecracker called a Lady Finger. It looked like a tiny blood-red cigarette. The safety meeting was over and the camera was rolling. The magnifying glass focused its plasma star on the tip of the wick string. Once both were held still long enough, there came a sizzling sputter, and then a sparkle. I was holding lit doom between my thumb and index finger but I could not let go. This tiny crackling sparkler had paralyzed me like some terrible Medusa. I was mesmerized by the monument of my situation. Clearly I had forgotten which button to push in my brain to release my pincers. I was screaming at the psychotic finger monsters on the end of my palm to let go. I knew the end was coming so my mind prepared its final testament. I left all of my belongings to the Tooth Fairy. I had done business with him before and we could cash in on all my bones. My folks would need that money to cover-up the shameful circumstance of my passing. "Here lies little Jimmy, too afraid to unfurl his fingers. He was killed by his own Lady Finger."

The wick finally reached its conclusive concussion. It set off a mushroom cloud of black soot and paper shrapnel. My entire being was shell-shocked in the sonic nightmare that had exploded between my fingers. I naturally assumed it had killed me. I was a ghost now, slowly unzipping the dirty coveralls of skin and bones. I asked my brother if he could still see me.

One morning, I found a wizard's wand pretending to be a coral snake. I was amazed it could be on the ground like this all acting completely normal. It wasn't in some fig tree or wrapped around a sacred boulder. It was on a steep red clay hill under sappy pine needles beside a noisy freeway. I wondered why a wizard was up here when he dropped it. I found his magic serpent wand coiled on the hillside. I decided I'd take it home to make it my apprentice. I tried to turn the snake back into a stick. I slithered every spell I could think of. I twisted my tongue like a snake charmer. I ever-so-slowly mouthed the words that told it to petrify. I sang it every sacred song of sleep I could remember. None of my tricks were working. It was a wizard's wand stuck on the magic serpent setting.

A boy named Simplicity came rolling down the hill yesterday. He plodded his way back to the top through a carpet of earthly feather. Bent green blades under his footsteps were resurrecting themselves to attention. At the summit, he waited till every one of them came full staff. Simple was ready to roll again. In his final breath, he stiffened his neck and crossed his arms like a dying pharaoh. The weight of death tilted his form over like a timbering tree. His feet flopped out straight as the momentum took his carcass rolling. Through squinted eyes he saw the blending of grass and sky. His eyelashes jousted an army of relentless green sabers. Every roll of his keel was an ambush of cheeky javelins. His mummy came to a stop at the edge of the river. He tried as hard as he could to remain perfectly still. He was dead after all. But from his motionless body a smile was resurrected. As crow's feet broke through the drawbridge, he laughed so much the grass giggled.

Look! I found a magic stick that runs on imagination. Use it quick to take over a castle, rescue a damsel, or stop a red ninja. It's shaped like a seven stretched high to heaven. It's the perfect ray gun with a thumbhole trigger. There's a scope if you need it, though your aim is impeccable. Your belt-loop is a holster and you cock it like this. Take these acorn smoke bombs and this wood-chip walkie-talkie. I'll be in the kitchen guarding the mothership on channel six.

Mother says, "Lord love a duck." So I tried to do that all summer. I had been feeding him corn allocated for a fish hook. The duck was white as snow and taller than a dog. He bore a bumpy orange beak and webbed booties. His long methodical quacks sounded like he had just told himself something funny. He was walking in circles chuckling like some fat guy with a monocle. He would show off and sit on top of the water. He'd sit out there all day bragging about it if you'd listen. I was completely in love with him. Day-after-day, I became more stingy with corn. I was slowly reeling him in like a big blue marlin. The day came when he was close enough to grab him. I landed dead center with my lightning quick bear hug. I remember the silky plume of his rump moments before I felt the torque of his neck. He was instantly displeased with my affections. His beak turned quick into a litigious cobra. He delivered a five-fisted death punch across my face and organs. His jabs were strategic and surgical. My merciless foul foe turned me into a bruised sack of kiwis and oranges. He waddled off in victory pumping his wings like a heavy-weight champion. I was surrounded by my own carnage of wet corn and drifting feathers. My summer wish was over and I wanted my mother.

I eventually emerged a new boy from my failed attempt at duck fishing. It was dusk and my brother had finished football practice. I remember how bright the overhead lights were on the field. I was in the back seat and poked my shoulders through the cockpit to announce something I had learned earlier. I asked my brother if he knew that we were both bastards. There was a sudden onset of gruff displeasure in the luxury wagon from my step-father. He almost seemed offended at this announcement. I was sent to the back of the cushion with no explanation. His eyes spied mine in the rear-view mirror between intersections. He was disappointed at my bewilderment. No one had bothered to tell me bastard was a bad thing. I thought it was a noble title like Duke or Liege. I was forced to abandon my new coat of arms as the Bastard of Lancaster Drive.

My next run-in with royalty was no better. It happened during my incarceration under a macramé owl lamp my aunt made. I was sitting across a thin line on a placemat from a Monte Cristo. I hated that sandwich and everything it stood for. It sat perched on pompous tall bread. The whole thing had been dipped in slug trails and deep fried in alligator boogers. That's how gross it was to me. I had just accused it of being corned-beef and was convinced it had been painted in some sick demented mustard. It stared back at me mockingly. Apparently, before I was born, I signed a blood oath of allegiance with my mother to swallow every wretched sandwich that was delivered to me. I would be required to fulfill my duties by swallowing. The Monte Cristo had nothing to lose which gave it all the power. I watched my enemy congealing before my firm protest. I tried pleading with it. I said I still had my whole life ahead of me. It sat glistening in my torture. Finally, as night fell over our battlefield, the Count was placed in the refrigerator to regroup in its own evil. The plate lifted off the table like an enemy spacecraft. It looked back at me and promised we would meet again tomorrow. I heard its menacing laugh over a crack of thunder from the ice-maker. I went to bed that night its cold prisoner. I held rebel council deep under the sheets. I turned the colored cotton patterns into a floor plan of the kitchen. I had till sundown the next day to plot my escape from the Count of Monte Cristo.

Even my dog could not save me. But he did hump a bully once. He was picking on me at recess and sometimes my dog would break free from our yard and come find us. This kid was picking on me at the four squares court and Jonathan came up and mounted him like a horny lobster. The kid kept telling him to stop but my Irish Setter's ruby red tail had its fill of him. The kid was pleading like I had been before my dog arrived. He was such a good boy. He always had your back.

He seemed to know which classroom I was in and would place his nose on the window to tell everyone it was playtime. At home, he would constantly bury my favorite stuffed animal. I would have to dig up Chewbacca in the yard or behind a row of bushes. I was a nine-year-old Dr. Frankenstein digging up cadavers after my four-legged undertaker.

As for the dead, I should explain how a plug of dirt the size of a finger had fallen from the Aldridge barn ceiling. The plug landed on top of the railing overlooking the old goat pen. All of us were certain it was a severed human finger. We called in one of the older siblings. Her forensic expertise as a sixth grader confirmed it was true. She told us it belonged to a child about our age. We took a roll call and none of us were missing. Yet here was the evidence. The finger of some fallen child sat there on the rail pointing at all of us as if we were next. For an entire summer the barn was off limits due to the open crime scene. None of us would perform a proper autopsy.

I had grown more rugged since then. There was a store called the "Handy Andy" and I was trawling the parking lot on my bicycle looking for a quarter. I wanted to buy a trick from Ms. Pac Man. I was going for a high score and needed energy. I found a can of Coca-Cola abandoned in a parking spot. It felt full, so I took my chances. I placed the hot thin metal against my open lips and dumped the contents on my tongue for its complete inspection. I closed my mouth fully around the carbonated discharge so I could immerse it in my blender. The cola fell under and around my tongue muscle long before I met the gritty gruel of spent ashes and crispy charred kernels. It accompanied the soft mush of paper filled with the stale soggy stench of spent tobacco. It was a bouquet of soot, fused in a steamy decanter of aluminum. Like a fine wine, it had been blooming on the hot black asphalt. I will never forget the vintage of hot coke with cigarette butt.

But it wasn't as bad as my first french kiss. I put my mouth around her pursed lips while she crowned her tongue out like a gopher. As I got closer it looked like a peeking dog's penis at a dinner party. Both of us were tucked inside a giant rubber tractor tire that had been buried in the playground. I wanted to go home so bad, but my own bike had brought me here. It was my first French kiss and this broad was ruining it. Who sticks their tongue out like a dog penis? I have been dared to do many things in my day. I have eaten tree bark. I have eaten tree bark with ants on top. I have eaten all kinds of construction paper with or without glue and glitter. I have never been challenged more than the time this girl made me lick her tongue tip. I got it over pretty quickly. I basically glossed over it like an armpit taking on deodorant. I gathered my clothes and exited the tire while she was snoring. I rode home stoically and took a long hot shower. I had just licked a peeping dog's penis.

My girl troubles had started a few years prior when I came face-to-face with a vampire. I was staying with my parent's boss for a whole week. They had a daughter, Jane. I never had a friend who was a girl before. It was going fine so far. I was playing with her Lite-Brite on the bed. If she warned me I did not hear her. The door burst open with a kick as she jumped out of her closet with no clothes on. She had tied a towel around her neck like it was a cape. When she landed she exclaimed in full nakedness, "I'm Dracula!" This was precisely when her dad walked in. I spent the next several days hiding in the basement in silence. I knew something bad had happened. I remember not having the courage to ask for details. It felt like I should have known and asking would only make it worse. The symbolism of the event in the bedroom was lost on me at the moment. It would be an accurate road map of what life had waiting for me with women. Every prop, costume, and circumstance in that room was poured and mounted on a bronze plaque reading, "Attempts to share light with women will be thwarted by vampires jumping out of closets." Jane was always nice though. I was too shy to talk to her after that. I don't mess with vampires.

I used to recite this poem very slowly and dramatically to anyone who would listen.

They call me Jimmy. Here I am. Cracking this corn.
And you. Where are you? You sit there. Acting like

*you don't care. But, I know you do. How could you
not? It is so early in the morning.*

Now this other kid named Bishop was trying to kill me.
We were boys on bikes and we were out on a cliff below
Point Park. I was leaning over the edge, dangling in the
vision of the Tennessee Valley. A huge log came whizzing
past my head and missed my ear by inches. I turned and
saw his cold milk-bottled eyes. He stood there, frozen, like
a gargoyle with shorts on. I was too ignorant to know
what he was up to. I knew he liked to play with me. Then,
a few weeks later at summer camp, we canoed to a
secluded island. Once we were on shore he began to hunt
me with a boat oar. The trees were close together so it was
hard for him. As he was chasing me he would not make
eye contact. He kept his vision always on my body where
he was aiming. I kept thinking if I could make eye contact
I could reach him. He was gone though. There were no
words from him. Just a sequence of grunting as his lungs
worked. He was the only one on the island. To him I was
a boar squealing. I made it back to the canoe and pushed
off shore without the paddle. By the time he had waded
out to me a witness was canoeing over. If I had died by
the cliff he would have pushed me over the edge. If on the
island, he would have pulled me into the water. I think
that's why he liked to play with me. I was fun to chase.

I got sick in a green, two-seated Jaguar when I was eleven.
My friend rode shotgun while I sat squeezed behind the
driver's seat. His dad had just bought it. I think he was a
newly single man. He was a jeweler and his Jaguar really

sparkled. I felt plugged into the back like an R2D2. He took us to a baseball game to route for the Lookouts. He loaded us with hotdogs and milkshakes. He drove us home up the "W" road. He was showing us the Jaguar's grip and acceleration. I felt fine right up until the event horizon. In a lot of ways, I was the last one in the car to know what was happening. I felt nothing and my body gave no warning. An octopus of chunk and essence jettisoned itself from my main intake. My brain directed the nostrils to provide auxiliary venting. A creature from inside my belly had spread its tentacles in every direction from all three of my head holes. A tremendous slippery steam-like haze descended upon the cabin. It sizzled like a smoking alien acid. The captain depressurized some windows and took us out of cruising speed. I was sad to see our fun end so quickly. I never saw that Jaguar again.

CHAPTER TWO

Choirboy

Speaking of dinner, I was in a tribe once called the Chattanooga Boys Choir. We sang a lot about dinner in the diner. We sang that nothing could be finer. We traveled the world singing about all kinds of things. We stayed in peoples' homes instead of hotels. We were forty-two boys from every kind of background. We climbed into a bus or plane wearing matching jumpsuits. We sang mass in Notre Dame Cathedral. One time we sang at Westminster for the Queen. I could have easily tackled her like a pro wrestler. She marched slowly by us in the ceremony as I told my friend what I was thinking. He laughed so hard she noticed. I stared her right in the eyes while she gave me her inspection. The Queen of England kept my stare while I considered my maneuver. The fate of the world was right there on my shoulders. My restraint had prevented some kind of terrible nuclear war I'm sure of it.

One night we arrived at a home in the Black Forests of Germany. Myself and another boy were given to an elderly couple for dinner. Their son, the only translator, was called away on something important. We were four gorillas grunting in the mist of two languages. I realized it did not matter what words I used when conversing. I could speak to them exclusively with my inflection. To prove this I held my spoon up and said, "These strawberries are yucky." They smiled back at me in full agreement as I patted my belly. We had a splendid time beholding each other's vibration and inflections.

After dinner, he invited us down a spiral staircase into the cellar. We spun past walls of wine bottle and brick until he opened a door that ended straight into a wall. At the bottom of this wall was a hatch you could crawl through. He pointed us down and through it. He jolted us in with tiny finger pulses of electricity from his excitement. He was scooting us in like he was in a hurry. We crawled through on our hands and knees into a wide room with a three-foot ceiling. The floor transmitted the cold through my kneecaps and palms. I crawled over to a lit tunnel from the ceiling. I was terrified from the anticipation. I wondered if the man had caught on about the strawberries being yucky.

As I stood up through the hole in the ceiling, my body grew fifty times higher as I overlooked the intricate landscape of a railroad enthusiast's vision. The trains were all running. They crossed bridges and waterfalls with real working fountains. They dove into tunnels like tiny steel dolphins. There was a town lit only from the flickering of tiny streetlights. Your mind could hear voices bustling in the tiny station. The mysterious delivery of this spectacle was truly impeccable. I understand now how language comprehension would have spoiled the entire presentation. He probably said in German, "Would you like to see my trains?"

There is a magical quality to first impressions. Sharing something new with someone is a sacred moment. Unrepeatable. A kind of virginity given. One Christmas I opened my presents early. The suspense had been building in a pile under the tree for weeks. I didn't know how to be in the same room with them. It felt like I was watching the most boring television in the world next to a time machine under a blanket in the corner. I opened my presents, played with them, they wrap them back again. This happened so often the house ran out of clear tape. I rewrapped them with electric tape from the garage. I believe my plan was to replace the tape once I found more. My mother was devastated because I had ruined her presentation. I took the virginity of the moment for myself and spoiled it for both of us.

In the summers the boys' choir would muster for two weeks in Sewanee Music College. We would wage war on the soccer field against season-old rivals. We were wild Indians in red and blue tank tops. The smell of cut grass made us thirsty for battle. We dined like victorious Vikings in shin guards. At dusk every night someone played trumpet. The sound of Taps against the melted purple of twilight rang into the rocks of our dormitory. Every morning we filled its chapel with the breath of living music. Songs older than this country echoing through a steeple in the mountains. We were a tribe of singers whose voice took us all over the world.

Ah, the things we can do with our hands. May your digits play a game of this little piggy. Up to ten and back again, let each finger push a button. Tell your thumbs to hitchhike across the ocean. Curl your pinky in a promise of allegiance. Chart your ring's courses through your golden commitment. Thank your middle finger for cursing the traffic. Watch your pointed steeple unfold itself into a church of fingers. Place your nestled candle inside these palms of cooperation. Let ten form one as a single light forges a congregation. This light of many is so much more than a finger could ever point to.

When I wasn't singing, I was a practicing ninja. I was in a Dojo of two people. Between my friend and me, we had a full ninja outfit. It was my night to have full custody. The boots were too long so my toes couldn't squeeze in the shoe tips. There was a lot of flapping noise when running. Life inside the headpiece felt like a steamed mummy in a black bathrobe. I was sweating halfway down my driveway. Still, I was dressed for a night out on the town.

I ventured down the block to see what kind of action a ninja could get himself into. I was nimble on the pavement. I would practice my silent footsteps in the wet grass under moonlight. I had no weapon till I reached the local golf course. The par four flag pin was a long striped quarterstaff. I could use it to pole vault across sand traps without leaving a track. I kept a television remote control in my chest pocket. I would creep near any window with a television and change the channel from the bushes. I would watch them struggle in frustration as I turned up the volume to maximum. I was an infrared nighttime silent killer.

By that time I was too big to be playing with toys. I didn't want anyone to know about it either. I kept most of mine stuffed in a tackle box and buried in an abandoned coal mine in the woods. If you took a flashlight down there, you'll see a lime green box with a sticker that says, "Decepticon." My favorite is the red truck named Optimus. He was an eighteen-wheeled yoga master and my rolling guru. I was ashamed of my passion for him. It felt the same as when traffic would catch me playing hide-and-seek in the bushes. I remember the embarrassment of being seen acting younger than my height was. It was the reverse of that sign at the roller coaster, "You must not be this tall to ride." Being conscious of how I looked or acted kept interrupting my vivid jam sessions of imagination. I did not want to consider what I looked like hiding behind the pine tree. I was trying to hide, not be seen. I struggled speculating about my own image from the other side of a stranger's car window. I wished I could stymie the growth of my height and my awareness. I tried everything to make it stop, from praying to wishing to pouting. I didn't know what was happening. I just kept crying under the house because something was taking my magic away. Every month I would imagine less-and-less.

In the summers we had a theater playhouse program. I would audition every year but usually was cast as human scenery. I was a fishmonger one year and the following year I pushed a cart but no one would tell me exactly what I was selling. I wanted to know my character's motivation so I decided it was turnips. I took all of my acting roles pretty seriously. It was considered dangerous for them to give me lines because I had on multiple occasions expanded them during dress rehearsal.

As my roles became smaller, I was often being called out for over-acting. I still don't know what they meant by over-acting but it was a majority opinion. I remember several times them discussing how to get rid of me while I was standing there. During a crucial scene in the Scottish play Brigadoon, an entire town and everyone in it was meant to rush off the stage in darkness so it could disappear into the mist. No one believed that my leg was asleep when I appeared alone in the spotlight on an empty stage with six fog machines gushing for me. The fog kept pouring so I decided to simply play dead. I imagined my character had died suddenly and the magic city left the body thinking it was organic furniture on the mountain. I remained perfectly still and committed with my eyes closed while the cast were shouting under their breath for me to exit. I remained for a while though because I took my acting roles very seriously. We couldn't have me just raise up from the dead now and walk off could we? I think that would be overacting.

In the eighth grade I began eating incessantly at lunchtime. Lunch was $.90 and I could borrow eight more dimes and eat twice; sometimes three times. I turned myself into an Olympic speed beggar and grew very chubby. I was trying to convince my dignity to find a different hostage. I saw it as this requirement to step outside oneself for inspection. I didn't want to go outside. That's where they grab you. I had yet to see an adult step outside and then come back in again. Adults didn't have much use for imagination. Well, they do, but they call it pretending.

I struggled for the next couple of years in school. I joined the cross country team to run from all the changes inside. I was the worst thing to happen to our team's running average. I would duck behind the grocery store or hide in the woods sometimes instead of running. Sometimes at races, I would run so slow the leaders from the second heat, the girls race, would pass me before the finish line. Most of my team called me "Orca." I guess that was the only whale name everyone could agree on. They would run circles around me and laugh at how slow I was. It was true I was a very slow runner. I would always agree with them about that. I wish I would have said "Orca" to myself more. I should have tried it on for size. If you listen to it, it is a really bad-ass nickname to have. It sounds way better than my last one, "Jimmy." It wasn't the name I hated as much as what was happening to him.

CHAPTER THREE

Student

I sold shoes in the mall at Thom McAn. I organized boxes in this magic dark hallway called, "the back." People would cast wishes for their favorite size and color. I would take their request to "the back." Some wishes were granted, some were refused. The back worked in mysterious ways. I don't remember her name or I'd say it. She was tall with the complexion of a camel. Her eyes were very sweet and trusting. She was so bashful it made her stick out more. I knew she had a crush on me. I relished in her fawning. Truthfully, I showed her no respect as a person. I never bothered to ask her story. She was the woman that's here to pump a palm frond in the background. As I said, I don't even remember her name.

Did I say I worked on commission? Because she would come in the store to find excuses to talk to me. I sold her a handbag once made of burlap. I filled it with all the charm I could squeeze from my tube until she bought it. I remember it was expensive because I made close to three dollars. She left the store with none of my admiration. I took it from her at the register. That night after the cage was closed on our main entrance, I learned to hate that job. I was in the back of the not-so-magic back, putting rejected wishes back into boxes, thinking about a person I just hypnotized into buying some burlap. I quit a few weeks later to pursue an opportunity with Godfather's Pizza.

Life-changing events rarely blink, "check engine." I was seventeen. My mission was to propel pies through space and time in under thirty minutes. Music exploded from my speakers. Hills bounced up-and-down as I screamed through the wind in a metallic blue wagon. Distance was the enemy and I was the destroyer.

He was maybe ten as life walked him home. His sticky feet clung to a brief and narrow shoulder. No homework caused his backpack to swing gleefully. In his mind beamed a lighthouse made of Fruit Loops and Scooby. His little tugboat had almost pushed himself home. One more hilly bounce and I came barreling behind him. My fender screamed the sounds of bloody murder as I squeezed the wheel like a petrified cobra. Stiff and straight from spine to brake I forged myself into a steel girder.

Somehow I missed him. Yet my mind recorded my heart and soul smacking him square with my bumper. My chassis sent his flesh-filled body sailing into a row of mailboxes. I could hear his baby sister screaming behind a front porch window. Her mother rendered wretched in a liquid pile of molten. I watched a father turned scarecrow hung inside a bag of skin stuffed with his own son's obituary. Life is so much more than a box of pizza.

Forever, I remember those inches. When life swiped its sizzling claws and I saw its fangs drooling with brevity.

I can tell you the 1984 Datsun 280Z was a pretty small car. If you don't know, it was a two-seater with a glass hatchback. That's why it seemed surprising to hear someone would rob a house in one - especially in a band uniform with a marching tuba in the back. The marching tuba is the really big one that looks like a giant donut. But that's what the police officer said when he pulled us over. He said we matched the description of two thieves who just robbed a house. One of us, and I won't say who, asked politely, "So two guys in band uniforms with a marching tuba robbed a house tonight?" Apparently that kind of thing happens in Red Bank on a Friday night at 11PM.

In fairness to law enforcement, I should mention I stole a car once. It was a five-speed turbo diesel made by Volvo with a sunroof. I was fifteen and it was Friday night. No one was home but me. I was stuck on the boring mountain again. I was drinking milk and eating fish sticks watching a show called Miami Vice on television. The thought of me alone, on a Friday night, watching Miami Vice with milk in my hand was crushing. The stallion inside me felt shame like he had never felt before. He needed more than fish and milk on a Friday. Quite suddenly, I left my house and stole a car. I had found its keys a few days ago and they were still hidden. It started right up for me like an accomplice and we pulled out into traffic. I was a cold steel criminal, drunk on the milk of turbo-powered freedom. I would never look back - at least for a while.

I drove to a quiet road to practice with the gearshift. The abandoned road had turned to gravel which then turned to dirt. I needed to turn around but there was not enough clearance to make a donut. I needed to put the transmission in reverse. I plunged my foot into the clutch pedal and grabbed the shifter like a saddle horn to pull the stick into position. I gave it gas as normal but the car kept lurching forward. No matter what I did or how hard I pushed, the vehicle would not go backwards. I decided I needed to cross a small stream to get to a clearing where I could turn around safely. I stepped out of the car and surveyed my stunt like Evel Knievel. It was maybe a foot deep at the worst. I decided I could make it. I got plenty of speed to plow through the water but as I came up the other side the right front end fell over the other side's steep shoulder. The car was thirty degrees downhill and teetering on two wheels at an angle. I could step on the back of the trunk like a see-saw and bring the vehicle back to level. I won't bother you with the rest of the story except to say the police were involved and the owner of the car was angry. It turned out to be registered to my mother.

Sometimes, I would park at the brow on Signal Mountain. Sometimes I would sweat past here on my bicycle in the summer. I would have deep conversations with friends here overlooking the city. I kissed a girl here lots of times. One night we saw a fire below us in the valley. I said, "Hey, my drama teacher lives down there, I bet she's awake." I waved down at her and joked how she probably didn't see me. Ms. Davis died that night in the fire. I waved as her world burn with no idea something like that was even possible. I might have even kissed that girl overlooking the fire. I couldn't tell anyone how awful that was because our teacher had just died. It seemed to be the least important part of what happened. Our drama class was going to perform the play, Grease. Ms Davis had given me the character Doody. I really felt like that afterwards. I didn't like going to the brow much anymore. What I hate most about death is its utter trivia. You would think the reaper would have more respect for his own craft.

Before that fire, I parked up here in the daytime in my dad's car. I had accidentally pressed the garage door opener for his office. The door was about twenty miles away but I had a clear line-of-sight from this vista. I wondered if maybe the click registered and the door had opened. I found myself wanting for a telescope. I took the remote out of the car and walked over to the edge and pressed it again hoping to close the door in case I had opened it previously. Realizing my mistake of moving the remote after the first press, I spent a few more minutes in a deep thought experiment. I finally pressed the button two more times before driving away exhausted from the entire experience.

I ran my mouth off to this guy at a party. He was picking on a girl who was seated at the kitchen table. I could gather easily how much she did not like him. I stepped in and humiliated him with my tongue. She was drunk and he was groping the integrity of her boundaries. I called him out in front of everyone over the party music. I took a live poll of his behavior. I put him on trial and someone actually slapped him. He left the inside of the party to wait for me on the outside of the party. I remained garrisoned till his curfew.

This brings us to the afternoon I was shooting pool with my friend, Erwin. He was a maestro of nine ball. His giant Polynesian body seemed to weeble wobble him around the table. He was finesse over fitness with a pool cue. His break was the electric crack of a whip from a precision steel hammer. He was a master hustler who never let on how soft he was. At high noon, my nemesis pushed through the swinging glass doors of Edsil's Game Room. He stepped into the saloon with a chomp and smack of his gum. He was slobbering at the sight of me across the length of two tables and the railing. He calmly saddled up to the bar to grab some change.

I broke my stick by unscrewing it and slid it back into the velvet sheath it came in. I zipped it shut and said it was time for me to hustle out of here. My nemesis met me in the threshold of my car door. He was sniveling as he flicked his blond bangs with the force of his own neck. He scanned me from optical lasers of hateful vision. He was reading my endocrine system for a flow of adrenaline and fear. He could see both of clearly as I told him I was not going to fight. He called me chicken shit and spit his gum at my chin. That was just enough to get him back his dignity.

Since my pool hustling career was not panning out so well, I decided I could be a bartender. The Brass Register had a long oak bar lining the north wall. It did have a brass register but we never opened it. During happy hour from four to seven, tall well drinks were half-off, and call liquor was a dollar cheaper. I handed Hank his scotch and soda with lemon. He was never consulted about the lemon. I just thought he could use one. If Hank was going to complain, it would be something far more important than lemon. Sometimes, he would complain about the scotch portioning. Sometimes we would get bottles that had too much space in the molecules. Hank stared at the world from thick drunk eyes and red cheeks a few nights every week. He was a stocky man with a crisp white shirt that made him taller. His long wavy hair was wiry gray, deliberate, and kinky. His tan made you feel like you were lakeside sitting on a red beer cooler.

Hank was once famous for suing the state of Tennessee on behalf of the snail darter. He was currently with the public defender's office where I was his intern and nighttime bartender. Hank was almost tactful. He carried it close like a tucked umbrella. All it took was a click of a button spring and it would rise in a slow slurp that ended with "kerchunk." This night, Hank's umbrella was missing. He was never a smelly drunk, nor an obnoxious one. Hank was an honest drunk. His fatigue would slip out from behind him and take over. It introduced itself in his verbal orders. You could see it in the long, awkward pauses. Some innocent point in space would be selected at random and he would stare it down like a pregnant zebra crowning. Sometimes he would just say my name and leave it floating. Tonight, he would speak that I had no business being a lawyer. If more words came out of Hank's mouth that night I didn't hear them. The entirety of the event was in one statement. I knew he was right. I would not be a lawyer. I didn't care as much as I expected. I had been programmed long ago by St. Elmo's Fire.

Chattanooga was still congealing back then. The river, like the city, was still dirty and the town was owned by people who liked it that way. One of these men was an island prince named Dr. Gonzali. I don't know the name of his island. Nor did I know islands even came with princes. He was a very tall, gauntly groomed gorilla. His shiny bald head popped out of a bird's nest of wiry black hair. His eyes were bloodhounds that hugged the ground like a vacuum cleaner. He was drenched in gold nugget and he bore a watch as big as a dinner plate that gave his arm a swagger.

Gonzali bought the restaurant to give himself legitimacy. In the afternoons a crayon colored Ferrari would slide into the loading zone so his entourage of arms and legs could pry itself from an Italian sardine tin. His driver was an elegant young female in a matching mini skirt. Thinking the best of her, I assumed she was embarrassed. The Doctor was always under the influence of some form of pharmacology. He was a doctor and he insisted it was strictly business. He considered the wait staff to be a personal harem. He brought a tequila belt bikini outfit in one night and started calling waitresses in the office to model it. He was King Kong on pills with a trust fund.

One night he was so drunk he tumbled down the set of metal stairs leading to the basement. His face was bloodied and pulverized and required surgery. I don't think he felt a thing when it happened. Within a few minutes of the ambulance leaving, one of the staff made a chalk outline commemorating his spilled body. She chalked out his drink and ice-cubes tossed a few feet away in the crime scene. They gave tours of her art installation to customers that knew him. He was famously hated and this fact never once seemed to faze him. He played the villain on purpose because he could afford it. I hung in as best as I could there while I finished my college sentence.

The plastic placard announced Philosophy, Room 226. Underneath, on a cut swath of white laser paper it read, Dr. Jacob Davids. He sat in a professor chair like an anti-rugged John Denver. His office was dark with no windows and next to the stairwell and atrium. It was a broom closet for dignitaries, with an placard. His name was Jacob Davids but the tape on the door called him "Doctor." He was my new advisor and he was about to ruin academia.

My previous mentor had retired without asking me permission. I called him Doctor but he acted the part. He was a wise man and he didn't need an office or a nameplate. We would talk in the stairway, under the skylights. We'd grab lunch and argue over how I had gotten so stupid. His challenges always swept me off my reason. But this new guy? He was a clown in a dark room, with a chair I bet isn't even made for a professor. It's probably a regular plastic student chair wrapped inside a sweater he got with suede elbow patches.

Jacob told me undergrads weren't meant to do philosophy. He said my idea was considered graduate or doctorate work. He turned a senior thesis into a long book report. My idea would die with him on his desk. I planned to challenge the litmus of reality against the internet. I wanted to prove that the web was its own universe; just as real as our own. I would do this using the very same proofs philosophy uses now. I had already documented which thinkers might agree with me. I would be challenging old ideas with this new world we call cyber space. I would be a philosopher for a semester and produce a written thesis and present it to my juried department.

But this is education not wisdom and Jacob wanted me to learn intellectual obedience. He wanted me to sit in a plastic chair with no sweater patches and copy scrolls from someone I pretended to admire. He wanted me to bore him with another biography of the same patron saints of thought. I was a monk in his monastery scribing him yet another ass-cushion so he could sit a quarter-of-an-inch taller in his plastic chair he covered with a sweater and suede patches. The experience of that man playing doctor ruined my academia. I have since discovered there are many more like him in the field.

After college I did find a teacher and his name was Charles. He was a photographer and a very good one. He kept a clean trimmed white beard with him at all times. His eyes were bluer than sunken icebergs. His ability to see was as fanatical as his personal traits. He taught me the secrets of the dark room. He taught me the secrets of stage and light. He showed me the chemical gnosis of exposure and timing. He was an alchemist of emulsion. He taught me the magic of scrying from a silvery salt water solution. Light surrendered to him in his studio. He was a painter of lenses and I was his apprentice. On his birthday someone mailed Charles a bumper sticker that read, "Suspected Freedom Advocate." Charles moved his van against the red clay hillside behind the studio. He placed the sticker on the rear door panel dead center. He produced a handgun and delivered three kill shots in a cluster. He said it made the sticker feel more authentic. You could tell he really liked his birthday sticker.

CHAPTER FOUR

Traveler

Quite unexpectedly, I found myself enlisted in the United States Navy. I was not as impressed as the sailor Billy Budd. I signed their form and told them to make me a sub-hunter. I was taught the ways of underwater signals and sound. They sent me to a base in San Diego and I became one of them. I trained to the call of whales in a sealed and secure air-conditioned building. To survive in a hive one must conform to its membership. After boot camp, this was tested on a trip to Tijuana, Mexico.

She was not cute, she was not ugly. She was probably just right for me. She sat on my lap and asked if I had fifty dollars. We walked outside the dark concrete bar into not so dark concrete. Every surface there was hard and painted, even the bottom half of the trees. We walked together, but not touching. She knew where we were going and turned us through a maze. I was lost, sober and rudderless so she taxied me up a flight of stairs and knocked on a caged window. An unnecessary delay occurred on the fat dark face that saw us coming. A slide from a small window opened where I was told to buy a five-dollar condom. I followed orders and the large metal cage door was swung open. Another mouse had made it into Shangri-La.

We entered a bedroom with corduroy green furniture. It was the softest texture my eyes could find. She asked something in Spanish. I shrugged my comprehension and grew more nervous since I could now see her better. She was thin; her body was the opposite of sublime. She wore a halter-top of tiny stripes whose colors were dull from their occupation. This cheap room was an automated carwash and I was here to get scrubbed.

She removed her top and I felt the floor move forward like a conveyor. Her shoulders were slowly dragging me in between two vertical motors spinning with bristles. I saw yellow dull flashing lights of her areolae as my hood got closer. I saw her humanity and it was enough to put the car in reverse. I complimented her equipment and told her I had to go now. She stopped me and placed her hand on my shoulder. She told me there would be trouble outside if I left. After some keen negotiating, we both concluded the only way I could leave was paying the full fifty dollars. A few seconds later she was grinning against the doorway with my money. The fat man was releasing the gate as I heard the two of them talking. His Spanish asked something. Her Spanish answered. They both laughed at me in English. I went down the steps like a slinky and found my crew without having to ask for directions.

Weeks later I would hear a thud so powerful it woke me up straight at three in the morning. If I heard anything, it was the sound of a giant sack of potatoes. Not to say the sound was loud as much as it was stirring. I knew someone had died and my sleep instantly evaporated. He had dropped from the third floor balcony. It was a drunken dead sailor. There was a short ceremony in the quad requiring dress blues. The guy who slept above me had the same problem. His stale, three-day-old beer would eventually ooze its way out his pores like a drip distillery. The chemistry of stale beer sweat would quaff my nose hairs every morning. I'd try and shimmy out of my bunk low to the ground like I was crawling though a house fire. But the next day for him was like the last day for the sack of potatoes. That night was another drinking ceremony for everybody that knew the deceased. Everyone said they drank to remember him. I think they did it to forget themselves.

The Chumpanzee

Stop. Release from your tongue. Step out of the skull with your hands up. See the pilots in your head. Look at all of those fancy gauges and frantic fingers mashing all the buttons. Who? Who? Ha. Ha. Chuckle at the chimpanzee buckled in your brain. See the desperate tooth marks adorn a toy plastic steering wheel. Windshield wipers swipe the truth from thundering wet bullets. He is hypnotized by the intermittent monotony of a squeegee. He is comfortable inside the cockpit. He taxis your skull out onto the billboard-infested freeway and snoozes on the cruise control of clarity's imitation.

After my retirement, I left from Springer Mountain on the Appalachian Trail. Two days north I met a rattlesnake. He seemed to be dead center of the trail but I never saw him. He hit me in the ears with the rattle. I was paralyzed by keratin ball bearings shaking in a chamber. My body was stalled in the standing position. It occurred to me that no one knew about rattlesnake hypnosis. They never bothered asking a dead person what happened. Even after I navigated around him, I found myself stupid from fright for quite some time. There was a resonance from this reptile that corrupted my thinking.

Years later I was camped in front of a fire near a commune in Tennessee. A late-night intruder pulled up in a four door Lincoln Continental. The blast of his headlights on high beam nearly blew my fire out. The car parked inches from my cowering flames. The driver shut off the engine and did nothing. He kept his lights on "fuck you" as they stared me down in full exposure. I was standing now but a bit hunchbacked. When I heard a voice speak from behind the wheel, it felt just like that rattlesnake. I was petrified in an instant. I felt the venom of his voice course through my sinew. I do not remember what he said. I was interrupted by a foreigner who came in and took over my tongue. A deep voice inside my stomach told him to shut his lights off. I could tell this voice wasn't asking. The Continental gave me a test with a long pause. I was so impressed with my voice I backed it up with my posture. That seemed to do it because he started up his barge and slowly backed away. I was so scared that night I wrote myself a lullaby.

May the sky be your blanket
the earth be your bed
In fear may these tree tops

slip over your head
You'll be cradled in moonbeams
and waterfall mist
The fragrance of cedar
to remember a kiss

A chubby brick church on the side of a state road had retired behind a chain-link fence with no gate. Its bricks were overrun with kudzu trespassing out of the basement storm drain. The plain plate glass windows were stained with chalky brown grease. In the yard, a plastic teeter caterpillar rose out of the ground from a rusty automobile spring. The church was previously occupied by a family of devote rodents who had found better accommodations. This forgotten brick temple was empty every Sunday. Inside, the ghost of a pipe organ played a eulogy for its congregation. On the front steps, once home to a fruitful wedding, rested a scratched and empty bottle of Southern Comfort whiskey.

The little temple remembered the day of the whiskey bottle. A white pinstriped Monte Carlo came rolling from the east. It pulled over abruptly right out front. The church was startled to see company on a Tuesday. Its lonely modest steeple rose quickly to attention. It could not wait to gift its sanctuary. A giant passenger door squeaked and creaked open from the push of a woman's bare leg on a flip-flop. A freckled mustard lady leaned out from her car seat and began to vomit in the gravel. The little church listened as she exorcised her confession. The driver fiddled with the air conditioning while his foot rested on the brake. He never bothered to put the transmission into park. Before they drove off, she held her finger up in a gesture of pause while she gurgled and rinsed her mouth clean with the last drops of Southern Comfort. She flung it as hard as her drunken arms would let her. It struck the door like Luther's hammer and bounced to the ground without breaking. She frowned and fell into her seat as the car kicked up an exodus of gravel. She left disappointed with the donation.

There is another sanctuary in Summerville, Georgia called Paradise Gardens. I had the occasion to sit many an afternoon with the good Reverend Howard Finster. I preferred not to speak during our visits as much as he preferred not to listen. We enjoyed sitting in a half circle of sunshine and silence while we waited for his porch to fall down. Howard's art was known far-and-wide as an artist. If I were to classify him fairly I would call it unabashed folk, quietly screaming, and unassumingly spiritual. His messages were powerfully threshed from familiar scriptures. He warned of rapture, repentance, and the folly of reason. He was constantly barraged with visitors wanting his hidden message. I was fine with just his carbon dioxide. He was kind enough to always give it to me. He pretended to recognize me long enough until I started to believe him. I would walk his rickety causeways of art and trinkets alone and listen to the wind play sunshine on my shoulder. I wrote Howard Finster a poem but never got to read it to him. I figured people show him enough of their visions already. Still, if you see him in heaven, please give him this next paragraph.

"Where are you?" I ask myself waiting patiently. Here I am with these plans of adventure. Toes flex and fidget at the hunch of missing you. I made us a picnic of apple and Gouda. We can divvy it with the knife we found crowned in the dirt. Remember that day? I was hot and you were beaming. We chuckled in the stream as we jumped rock and boulder. Everywhere we looked I saw your reflection. I needed you that day. I always need you. You are my reason to rise from my pillow. When you leave I collapse and dream of the pretty pictures you gave us. I am your helpless child, your suckling young infant. You show me my shadow and remind me I am seen. On closing my eyes I can feel your light's whisper. My eyelids are no match for your mighty burn. Sear through this fog that lies between us. Let me bask in your glory and walk in your way. You are my sunshine, my only sunshine, please come out and play.

I would not have assumed I was an artist when I met Howard Finster. I did not possess any sense of spectacle then. I simply felt closer to normal when I was around him; less unfitting. Howard the person was not a spectacle either. The part he liked the least was all the discussion. As if his art wasn't speaking for itself already. They would look for secret messages in lines of paint that were already written. They were pretending to read a puzzle from a spelled out bible verse. Pretentiousness is the anti-thesis of folk art. So sayeth the Good Reverend Finster.

CHAPTER FIVE

Nendawen

I was finding my identity easier in the wilderness. Two days ago, I came here to visit the land called Savage Gulf. The worst storm of ten years decided to join me. It was my first solo trip with a backpack. I spent the first day diving from boulders into a mountain lake with beautiful strangers unashamed of their bodies. Yesterday afternoon was as peaceful as the morning is now. I had staked a fresh campsite high on the southern ridge top. Black beans and white rice were boiling together on a stove. The calm canopy had joined me for dinner. It was the place you might catch someone whistling.

And a zipper in heaven did rupture. The ground around me turned into a mudslide. The pot filled with rain water in seconds. It knocked over the stove, which pierced the fuel canister, which set the fire that would not go out. In seventeen seconds the world I knew before was over. I spent most of that night crouched on my ankles; in a tent stuffed with water, in a show of fire, lightning and thunder with the crashing of trees all around me.

I emerged in the morning, stunned and soggy in the gentle sunlight of dawn. With shivering arms, I pack my wet, melted campsite. I salvaged a granola bar from the disaster and slid it into my pocket. I have it now for breakfast overlooking this savage gulf. I have never felt more alive than this morning. Sighing down into the valley now that my troubles are finally over. What a night it had been. As my fist formed around an empty wrapper, the sound caused something at my feet to quickly coil. I saw the shape of a snake with diamonds on its back. Its head was a pointy throbbing arrow. The hull of my body instantly retracted my feet like landing gear and took off as fast as the hydraulics would let them.

And a Cloud did come Crashing

A flight of fluff fell under the weather
Surely the heavens did grumble
But earth stood still in her steadfast
Swords of thunder ripped open the sky
A stab of arrow pierced sky's thin rice paper
The brave ground gave no worry
I see a rabbit finding shelter
A radar nose twitches the forecast
Birds settle in to preen on my windowsill
The salon of chirping means all is well

As time passed, so did my travels. I found a town and came upon its center. It held inside it a proud courthouse of steps and gray stone. It stood adorned with a single Latin oath to justice that loomed heavily over a rod-iron entry. Its plot of land was hunkered in grass and flanked by park benches. The field of green was pinstriped by cobbled sidewalks. Plaques of bronze sprouted paragraphs to be pollinated by the eyeballs of visitors. The steady growth of progress over the years raised the buildings around it like a shower curtain. I sit to watch all these people unanimously coming and going. Giant oaks spring up from the ground to shake each other's hands in public. The good business of squirrels here is booming. My ears record a quorum of blue jays passing amendments. I find myself surrounded by pigeons busking for popcorn. I must be the only one here who forgot his agenda.

Days later, I was starting to feel silly. I was at a crossroads around midday, waiting on a squirrel to make up its mind. I had promised I would follow him. GPS had not been invented so I was flying solo. It was a lonely gravel road with plenty of time and shade. He was clearly in no hurry either. I finally had to turn my motor off. I had found this squirrel at this intersection quite by accident. The map showed a town called Love's Hollow and I had to see if it was true. I never did find that place. I don't know if it is true. I decided the squirrel would be nature's way of giving me directions. That was about seventeen minutes ago if I was counting. I almost honked at him but I knew that would only take me to karmic trouble. I was a laughing hostage to a promise I made to a critter in the middle of Tennessee. He went west eventually. I thanked him and did the same. About twenty miles later I ended up at a wilderness camp for juvenile delinquents. They said if I could last twenty-four hours they would hire me as a live-in counselor. I left a year later a much different person thanks to the directions from a squirrel.

I was Mr. True. We were Nendawen, the torch bearers. After the cold winter, Johnny brought me a carved staff of red cedar. It had the burrowed journey of worms etched all over its body. It stood tall and proud like I did when I held it. It bore the mark of our tribe and designated me as their leader. It was the most sacred thing I had ever been given. It felt like it smelled in the hand. It had been waxed and shined with love and attention. It was adorned with a lone white turkey feather. When I saw it, I knew Johnny loved me like a father. The next day, a boy named Squirrel asked to see it. He knew how much I liked it. He smiled at me before he beat it into splinters against a tree stump. When I saw this, I knew he loved me like a father, too.

Dale found a dead raccoon. He wanted its tail and I could not think of why he should not have it. "No" was not an answer then for he would hold me accountable at group fire. So we brought a shovel, long loppers, and prepared a site near the body for burial. I was not going to let Dale touch it. I decided it needed to be me. I drug the carcass into the pit and laid it on its back so it could see me. I pushed some cool dirt around its body like I was tucking it in. I slid the loppers around the crest of the tale to cut it. All it lacked was a simple press to free his prize. But I could not do it. I looked at Dale and said, "What if he still needs this?" Dale filled the hole with dirt and we returned from the burial empty-handed.

One night, I took everyone's names away. We each wrote our name and threw it into the fire. We stepped back into the trees and watched each other's past burn as if they were strangers. They were now. We were reborn. I would not let them back into camp until they chose another. I painted their foreheads with the ashes from the fire. They came at me with names that were wild horses. They said things like "Red Arrow," and "Turbo." Once said he was "Thunder-Buttkiss." Together we learned the power of resurrection. We burned our past to start over. When they left Three Springs to return to the florescent world. I gave each of them their name back. I told them it was all better now. Their name became a source of honor. I wiped their faces again with the ashes of their last fire. Then I cleaned it all off with a wet towel. I told him he was a man now, cleaned by the forest. They will always be my children.

To do my job, I had to learn the ways of wilderness safety. They sent me to Nantahala and I was reborn again in the river. A wild, topless woman said "let's go" and I followed. We were together for a week studying each other and wilderness safety. She was my safety buddy and she really showed me. I climbed in her kayak so she could buckle me in for my lesson. She stretched my skirt around the rib of the boat until it was taut like a drum. She climbed in her boat and pushed herself off into the current. I tried to follow her as gracefully but my boat rolled the moment it hit the water. I lost the paddle as soon as my shoulders dunked. My head was submerged and my helmet slipped over my eyes. I was flowing blind, down the river, upside down and backwards. I tried to free myself from my awful decision by pulling a release strap. In the darkness, I kept tugging but nothing would happen. My head is colliding with boulders as I keep gaining speed down the river. My mouth becomes a screen door in a submarine. My arms start clawing for the slippery rocks on the bottom. I am trying to pull myself up onto shore. I try for the strap again only this time I find a different one. In one exaggerated yank, It pops me free and water rushes into the boat. The shock of winter is all around me now. My core yields enough energy to pull my lower self out of the canister. My hips will not disengage. I am married to an upside-down boat full of water. As my face runs through the river stone cheese-grater, I am reminded a topless woman insisted this would be easy. I felt destined for the happenstance of bottom feeders till I finally emerged in an evolution of adrenaline. I crawled myself from the freezing ooze like some primordial land fish with a ridiculous plastic tail. My vision was still covered by my own helmet. My mouth was gaping like fresh fish gills on a cleaning table. My safety buddy was fifty yards down river hovering in the current. She was as nimble as a water spider wondering why I didn't just flip myself over. She yelled me her last question as safety buddy, "You okay?"

Dawn's Song

Grey and green, not black and white
My heart a stone if you hold too tight
I watch the dawn put her sky to bed
Been up all night with her eye so red
I feel your trunk; it's wide and strong

Breathing tree take me along
Won't you raise me up my friend
I want to see her rise again
Sometimes blue, but always green
We wash our hands to feel the clean
Head to my chest, I whisper you
Deep in your dreams, I don't get through
Something sacred when I'm alone
Call your name on that psychic phone
Kiss on your head, telepathy
I'm calling you please answer me

When I woke up in the forest, the first thing I heard was a whistle. The birds were ten tasks deep into their agendas. I am a lazy caterpillar slowly chomping my mouth like a eucalyptus. My shoulders slowly convulse in the drama of my stretching. I wonder where I am as I peek out the sliding van door that's still open. My eyes are immediately dancing in the menagerie of a cobalt disco. Last night I seemed to have parked on a geyser of butterflies. My toes could not touch the ground in all the flapping. I lean my head and shoulders out instead and bask on this lake of electric blue wings. Hundreds of solar motors all flapping in idle. They have parked their toes in the mud to act as anchors. Their wings pulling themselves off the ground while their feet sit stuck in the earth. I am a ginormous caterpillar snoozing in the middle of butterfly aerobics.

CHAPTER SIX

Fountain City

It was Independence Day and I had left Mark Twain forest from loneliness. I came upon a tribe in St. Louis called the Grateful Dead. They were kind and we knew each other for some miles. I heard their chief Jerry Garcia play with his nine fingers. I met dirty entrepreneurs busking grilled cheese sandwiches on the sidewalk and joined them. I made a sign that said "Tennessee James' Mushroom Quesadillas." I sold them all like hot cakes. People kept asking if they were psychotropic. I kept saying, "I don't know, you tell me?" I confess here they were Portobello. But people claimed they felt amazing. I think it was the garlic. I was grateful to meet this new tribe. I was sad to see Jerry go so soon after I joined them. I kept on west with my tribe of one again.

In a coffee shop, in a city, a young man in his twenties was telling a young woman what it had been like to be chubby. He made assumption after assumption she was listening. The vibration from his vocal chords ricocheted off her torso and bounced into her notebook. He watched her stare right through him.

He sighed audibly to indicate a conclusion to his presentation. He nestled his chin between some fingers he had available. He didn't mind her silence. He found pause on her forehead. It was his favorite spot to perch. He turned himself into a happy raindrop rolling down her temple. She blinked slowly from his reverence. She was preoccupied but still basking in his worship. The pencil she fondled helped her inventory the room. She was counting the heads she could take for breakfast. He watched her eyes slice each one like a melon. He was glad she hadn't been listening. He would have been wise to leave the table but there was no place he'd rather be.

Outside the window, two pigeons jousted over an English biscuit. There was a sense of equilibrium between them. Neither was too invested in the opinion of the other. Each stab of the beak was forceful but somehow unselfish. It was choreography to him. He concluded they must be a couple. They met on a wire dangling from Walnut Bridge in the springtime. The sun was setting, she cooed, he gurgled. It was love at first flight. And here they were years later getting fat on each other's company. He smirked at his envy of pigeons.

As it turned out she had been listening. She heard every word he sent her. She had been quiet from wondering if she was pregnant. Her detachment from the idea felt like maybe it wasn't true. Surely, she would "know." She imagined her molars resonating. She combed the front of her teeth with her tongue back-and-forth. She wondered if the tiny foreigner in her basement could hear what she was thinking. She decided the conversation was none of its business.

She took his bait and diverted her focus to weight. Would her pregnancy be a prison? Why wasn't she freaking? She wanted to tell him. She needed to know for sure. She sat up straight and closed her sketchpad as if to announce a new policy. Her eyes met his face knowing it would make him stop talking. He stopped talking. She said nothing as he began to pack up their belongings. She decided this was none of his business either. He was not the father.

She pretended to prefer books. She bore the name of an astronomer. She was highly intelligent and consistently disappointed. She considered herself global. She liked to say, "Mahogany." She saw most of the world through windows in her nostrils. She bowed to those more arrogant than herself, though rarely did this happen. She kept a pet cello in her closet. She professed a deep love for it so she would barely touch it. She was a symphony of pale skin brooding in a corset. I played her juicy thin reed like an oboe. I had never been so deeply in love again.

As it turned out, a man named Doug had been watching us from her balcony. She must have known he was out there. I imagined how much fun it was for both of them to be on the higher ground of a secret. They pretended to be a couple that was over. I was the new kid in town. It was two rats having fun with a mouse who had never seen a love triangle. The experience made me buy a banjo.

Ballad of a Rooster

If the sun refuses to rise

My old friend rooster will die
I'll be seeing him as soon as I am at
The place I call my Tennessee
My darling won't let me call her mine
Till I got down on my knees
My love for her was strong as old moonshine
And sadder than the fallen blueberry
If my lungs refuse to take breath
My heart would surely cease to bleed
The way I'm feeling now that ain't so bad
I'm sadder than a weeping willow tree

The October sun burst through my window like a proud laser. And in my den, thus spake hibiscus. Its leafy hands stretched up like a child begging to give his answer. I noticed it missing the sunlight by inches. It had been missing this manna for weeks now. There it was, inches from the glow, stuck in a pot of shade. From its jail of shadows, it could see the floor planks basking. And there I watched, a guilty warden. Redemption let me sit down beside him. I pulled my knees close to my chest as the floor spoke to the chill of the morning. Down here, the hibiscus was my brother. I sat with my new friend in his foxhole soaking up the scene. We would wait for the sun together.

At first, it felt like church with the parents and the sleepy ritual of praying to some Saint Elsewhere. I settled into my pot and let my daydreams spread out like grazing buffalo. I was sharing a pew with hibiscus. Sitting with him, I noticed something unexpected. A deep calm rose out of my immobility. All of the decisions of where to go and how to get there faded to nothing. Glued to the floor, the world becomes a giving canvas. Like a slow song played even slower while passive miracles ebb and flow in the living room.

I told myself, "Hush." The sunbeam is about to sing its solo. As my day spreads out before me, I imagine life from a bucket of soil. The conversation in my kitchen was a land far away. I could hear the coffee pot sputtering. But perhaps it was nothing. After all, there was no kitchen.

The city is quiet in the dark as I lookout for the pirates of Kansas City. I am perched on an outdoor sofa, overlooking a brisk night from my top floor balcony. Across the block, I watch a SWAT team discretely loading tactical gear into a bread truck turned assault vehicle. It is 4am and time to make the donuts. They are pillaging for criminals on the concrete waters in their aluminum Black Pearl. I can smell the adrenaline from here. They are fully engaged in the moment. This is what they live for.

From that same crow's nest, on another brisk night, I had just returned home on foot. I watch what could have been my slaughter as a gang of thirty bicycles comes gliding into my concrete harbor. Their sound is a chorus of whirring atop the stretching of metal linkage. Each crank of the pedal is an oiled gnarly tooth clenching around a sprocket. The fear of this hive bounces back and forth inside my chest. I relax my face to dissipate. The armada of teenagers owns the harbor now. They spread out into circles to prove it. They would have sniffed me dead down there a moment ago. The safety of nothing is between them and me. I am simply elevated and in the dark like a crow on a pedestal.

I never told her that I loved her. I did tell her I was hungry. She knew exactly what I meant. She was a feast of power. I lived above her in a building of six houses. It was the only time she ever looked up to me. She was a triple water sign, whatever that meant. I only flooded her apartment twice though. The first time was my shower; the second, from my kitchen. I won an Oscar playing her dolt. Years later, I sent her a poem but all I could write was "Annie is." Enclosed was a garlic stem I thought reminded me of her. Her gaze felt like cool cucumbers and rippled my soul with color. When she left, our poor building missed her.

Paint would dry as I snailed myself across her landing. Sometimes, I tempted her door with a cushioned tap of two fingers. I did it like a double-dog dare between two children. Her portal of oak was as solid as the ancients. I knew it would open if I had a good reason.

One bright day, a stone lion was basking outside an insurance building. I decided to sit on its back and watch the people. It was the afternoon, and it was sunny. I whispered to the king of the concrete jungle, "Tell all of them to wake up." I dismounted the cat and walked towards the road when a driver yanked his car out of the river. Bewildered, he beckoned me over to his passenger window and began asking me questions. "Hey, how's it going?" He told me something made him stop. He didn't know why or what. I told him he is learning to see the shadows. I ran home to deliver her my fresh catch.

Knock, knock, and knock. I was panting. I should have caught my breath first. The door opened fourteen-point-two inches. My chest announced, "My will stopped traffic." The door opened completely from her gesture. She smiled and nodded and seated me on a speckled carpet as she poured foreign tea for my belly. My lips tasted pepper and cherry from rustic petals of silk and oil. She listened to me fill her living room with the stone lion. I could tell my moment was Annie's constant state of existence. Even her dog was a wizard. He stared at my mouth while it moved with a very respectful pity.

One day, while barefoot, I kicked a raised slab of concrete. Deep chords of pain began a steady pounding. I hobbled home squinting through a cracked wet face. As if waiting for me, she came outside and sat my body down on the porch. With crisp blue eyes she directed her hands together breathing into them. A conch shell of fingers created a sweat lodge in her palms. The energy in my foot was pounding its drums for her. I know she could hear them but she was waiting. She required the anticipation for her elixir.

She wrapped plasma mittens around my toe and began a conversation. I never heard a word. My foot was lost in her verse. Her hands had come to listen to its throbbing. The pain stopped making so many objections. It seemed to open up and tell her all about the concrete accident. They both agreed it was a misunderstanding. While orange magic poured from her olive fingers, I convinced her she was amazing by staring at her. I stopped my pen on "Annie Is."

Catch my Drift

If I call your name, with the silence speak
If I draw your face, will it come to me
If I stay with you, will you go away
If I learn to love, must I learn to hate
If I cut you loose, will you set me free
This can't be the way, love supposed to be
If I loose my crutch, can I stand up straight
If I see the hook, will I take the bait
Should I be alone, to feel real and safe
If I play the game, must I leave the base
If you catch my drift, we can sail away
If you want to roam, know that it's okay
Happiness ain't free, with a ball and chain
Time like clouds will roll, we can't stop the rain

There was a rainbow gathering deep in the forest of southern Missouri. Our entourage had dismounted from the vehicle. Car doors clunked closed as government rangers in tall hats loitered nearby waiting for hippie carrion. They sniffed our party behind their thick sunglasses but the canopy was calling and we had come in peace. Water bottles capped full and hung from bandanas. Like wet peaches, the forest swallowed us effortlessly.

Miles of branches acted as turnstiles leading us to the edge of a makeshift village. The first child I spotted was a tall man in his twenties. He wore nothing but a studded collar and sagging tighty whities. He was chained to a tent stake and had committed himself to the role of being a dog. I knew he was a child of the rainbow. I passed his pen like a silent cat not looking for trouble.

Our group dissolved without notice as each of us sat in a private buffet of vision. Crossing a stream, I heard girls singing. One was knee-deep in trench mud and cleaner than all the rain. Ahead lounged her sister picking flowers. She was pregnant and stunning. A single swath of cloth covered her entire body as daisies pooled in her fingers. Ahead, a fat man nestled in a congregation of people kept repeating as if they weren't getting it, "Be Here! Now." His walking stick poked holes in the ground like a woodpecker. Everywhere I looked was a child of the rainbow.

That night our fire burned big as a mountain. A circle of drums came booming in like thunder. My soul rattled itself loose from its seatbelt. I saw the tribe's rhythm soar so high the moon curled its toes to not get wet. We were all one and I had become nothing. All my wishes cooked true in the ascension of sparks above me. In a sudden crescendo, my chest erupted into a raging volcano of howling. I was reborn a naked werewolf of the rainbow. I remember running naked under the moonlight. No one saw the old me ever again.

With heart free my words drip from a pen. From a mountain of consonants I vowel at the moon. I hunt stories in the crook of my fingers. I am a caster of light through a prism of letters. My photons land in your chest like throwing stars. Feel my mood through your thick dark bark. Our touch is a circuit.

She told me frankly, we were nothing special. My youth recalls the feeling as I paced through the streets at night. Gut-struck by a punch felt deep down in my intestine. My breath shattered and scattered into a million pieces. My back bends like a knee as it searches for any kind of rhythm. I am drowning in the surprise as my heart gasps for a raft. Now I am stranded on this sparse island. Vultures circle my hope lying fetal and panting. My destiny revealed in a feeble shadow. I am stretched across the dunes as the sun is slipping away again. And in the dusking quiet, I note the moon has my company. She is up there, deep in our mood together. She reflects a burning passion from a lover. Pools of tranquility looking down on me with sweet pity. She said to me that sometimes, the stars don't twinkle. They pulse an S.O.S. but you don't listen. Across the thick dark sky, in this cold, in these bones, I am my favorite hermit. I wrap my fish in the news of dead bodies. I spark my tinder from an old message in a bottle I had been saving for later. The hurt that burns me warms me now in a sandy bunker. I paint my forehead and cheeks with the black ashes of this fire. It burns as bright as my lonely heart's drumming. Through my nose, and out of my mouth, there was no need for resuscitation. I am alive and feasting on regret's bloody throat. Healing is so overrated. Scars are noble trophies. Memories are ribbons. Yours to me is velvet blue with a giant gold medallion. It says "First Place in Boring." You should be so proud of me.

I came back to my hometown of Chattanooga but no one noticed. I came back to find that I had already been forgotten. I called up my professor but even he did not seem to remember. I tried to make us both feel less awkward by saying my face would ring a bell. My wax was melting and the world wanted me down from the clouds. I thought I left this town years ago but it was the town that left me. I explored my way up the bluff to a statue of Icarus leaping out over the river. His bronze face was windswept and determined. He was telling the sun he really thought he could make it. Like me, it was the wax that did him in. Man's body is reality. His wings are dreams. The wax is the alchemy that holds them together. We are all shapers of wax. We wax above the clouds or wane on the side of the cliff; watching a town float downriver.

CHAPTER SEVEN

Asheville

I went to Siler's Bald in Nantahala for a few nights on the Appalachian Trail. I had burned a piece of my Navy uniform because I was free now. I drove west towards the Tennessee valley. The day was clear and I had no problem seeing the police car pull me over. He asked for my driver's license and held it up like a game of trivial pursuit and administered a pop quiz. He asked me for my date of birth which I told him. He asked for my street which I told him. He asked my age and plain as day I said, "twenty-seven." I saw his lips pressing buttons on his calculator. He accepted my answer in the confidence it was given and awarded me an expensive ticket for speeding. I returned to civilization and was cleaning up in the shower when it dawned on me that I was twenty four years old, not twenty-seven. Either we both subtracted wrong or I had exhibited some sort of Jedi mind power. I should have told him I wasn't the speeder he was looking for.

I pressed my knuckles deep into my eye sockets and turned my eyelids like they were doorknobs. I was trying to wring my brain out. I wished to carve out the parts that caused their awful vision. Moments ago, I was in a forest laughing. We were playing on a thick rug of moss under sequoia so tall the stars knew their name. The bark was soft and conformed to the press of my fingers. We were hunting by firefly after the sun left its throne. A light fog lingered over the ground at waist level. Our prey was the freshly fallen buckeye. We gathered them up by the armload and peeled out their shiny centers. The youngest sister Pandora was our basket and she was spinning and laughing so much she could barely stay straight. An endless line of children was emptying their cache into her dress as she spun like a record. Underneath the linen, her arms had formed a hoop basket. She was chock full of buckeyes and giggling out of control. Someone mentioned a kangaroo so she started hopping. With every jump her bounty leapt out like a hundred dolphins hanging in the air. The hollow click of nuts crashing down on each other sounded like sea foam. If only it was over.

A magnetic charge of static filled the forest. The fog around us boiled instantly into steam. Ears and eyes rose in terror as everyone scattered like deer. I remained, frozen by our spectacle. I was in a trance as I witnessed tall dark figures appearing behind curtains suspended in the forest. One materialized directly in front of me. It was nine feet tall and had no neck. I was looking at a chest with a clump on top. Every feature was dark and muted. His stature blocking out all light as I shrank tiny inside his shadow. He lifted me by my neck effortlessly with one arm. My limbs dangling like a dead rabbit and he kept my skull aimed into his mouth like he was catching ice cubes from a cup. He was forcing me to look into him. He was milking my reaction for an expiration date. I can't tell you what his face was made of because of a cold green light implanted on his forehead. He was a stalking Cyclops framed in a steaming hot alien shadow of stinking rot.

He revealed a device from a pouch that looked like a jumbo electric razor. Each side of the instrument had pincers like a beetle. He held it inches from my chest and waited to make its adjustments. They found their mark and I heard a whir and a hum. Two bright blue electric bolts dove into my chest just outside my collarbones. I felt wire-thin electric bolts burrowing into my skin. They hijacked my chest muscles and I was no longer commanding my lungs. My captor seemed to perk up with the rising of his meter. The machine began its evil cycle by expelling my lungs completely. My chest sank deeper and deeper as I felt the suction fold my ribcage. I was as terrified as the creature was successful. He turned a dial again and my mouth flung its flap open from the gush of new air and suction. I had no control of when or how I was breathing as he collected my terror like pollen. He drew himself closer. I could taste his thoughts in my mouth now. The machine was on autopilot and it was drinking me like a slaughtered cow. My dangling feet finally stopped pleading as my will gave in. I was fully broken and lightly convulsing.

He had tapped my prana like molasses behind tree bark. I watched him adjust another dial and somehow understood he would let me go. I was overcome by the premonition until I realized I was remembering. All of this had happened before, and before that, and before that.

The pincers released their thick bolts from my chest. I felt pinholes in my skin sear themselves closed. I was breathing on my own as I struggled to catch any rhythm. The device scanned my forehead and temple. I remembered it was going to erase my memory so they could return to feed again. I heard a hum erupt from the device. I had to warn the others. I had to find a way to re-

I have a box of snapshots taken from a Christmas parade. Glossy smiles I caught perched on a horse and buggy. Groundhog-like people rising out of a den of blankets waving wishes and throwing gobs of candy from a bag. Let's hitch our wagon to their enthusiasm. We don't need a ticket to dangle feet. We are hobos on a lovely train catching smiles with our camera. Keep waving while I hold open the shutter. Here, I give you a perfect grass saber. Squeeze it taunt, like a reed and blow it a firm kiss. The kazoo of green zaps storm clouds from miles away. See the eyes of our horse watching? He can feel the weight you saddle. Be sure and think him a tale of love dipped in happy. He will carry us proudly through this line of festive poinsettia.

In my garden on Pluto, I think back to a love that was a tempest. So deeply chemical. Molecular. Some pages I just can't turn. Or at least it sure seems so. It's like that giant stone in the garden that has to go. I can't seem to slide my fingers underneath to get a grip. Tendered fingers clawing through muddied sharp gravel. Where is the bottom of it all? How deep, wide and heavy. Once there, I'm sure I can pry it up. Longing for that satisfying dramatic slurp as mud's glue gives way to my hoping.

Perhaps this garden should flow around it? I again grab the hose as if it was a new idea. "Let the ways of water loosen up this madness." The cat perches nearby wondering who I am talking to. Thumb to spout, I focus this stream into a laser. Through the gushing, I remind myself of the whole story. How she drove sixteen hours to surprise me. Boy that sure worked. I sent her off with some chardonnay and a stupid story about Pluto. If there was a song "The situation was different" it would have played in the background. Years have passed, but never that night. Today, it kicks me still. I found her single in the Fall. She tells me there is nothing left to say. Her phone rings empty. No funny stories. I stand a man convicted of loyalty. How cold it is, out here with Pluto. At one time, we were both considered something. We both chuckle in our orbits. Perhaps it is better this way we say to each other. I feel daisy's push as I return to digging. I wave a magic finger as the moon draws closer. She whispers, "The thing about pages is you only have so many." I retort in jest, "Oh, be quiet moon and hand me that shovel."

Time has a big mouth. You can see its crusty molars and shiny fillings. Time flaps a tongue with bumps as big as boulders in a virgin field. Time cuts our guts out and leaves them hanging. Time can never be trusted with a secret. You can be nice to time but it will not return the favor. We give it rides on our wrist. We dote on it daily. We make sure to always follow. My mom keeps it in a bottle on her desk in the kitchen. She turns it every so often to watch the pouring of sand. I go home to visit and we play with it in front of the fire. Finding words in a box as time burns itself away in the hearth. We cook with time, we drive it places. We praise its lumbering achievement. We announce its arrival with a ding. We mark it with appointments. We give it every second of our focus. We pay it by the hour and ask nothing in return. Time surrenders itself like an elephant.

The first time I saw her she was swinging from a branch like a monkey. She bore the elegant angles of a supple ballerina in work boots and corduroy. One night, I serenaded her with a bamboo flute for what felt like an hour. She was behind the window, nested in her couch like a robin, not hearing a word of it. I should have brought an amplifier. Oh the pain of double-pane windows. I gave a knuckle solo which she like enough to let me in. If pumpkin pie was any sweeter they'd call it Audrey.

She buried her eyes like a treasure chest in a pillow. I waited for those pupils like it was a sunrise. We play peak-a-boo in a tent for two. Early today a butterfly blinked on a shoulder. I felt the flow of cold crystalline as tiny fish mingled with floundering toes. As love filled my cave I yearned for the drowning. Make my sorrowed skin turn crisp like empty cicada. As my fingers make camp in the valley of her spine. Gone are all the hungry coyotes. Tonight this fire crackles in our nudity. May a wind come send our sparks up into the firmament. A tale of two flung light speed from a campfire.

I lived downtown in a big art studio. It was nighttime. I wanted to be outside. I wanted to feel naked. I wanted to feel vulnerable. So I took all my clothes off before climbing the ladder on the outside of my building and up to the roof. I got to the top. The stars were out. I was downtown. It was nighttime. I was outside being naked and vulnerable. It was glorious. Two police cars pulled in and parked beside the ladder. They hung out in their cruisers for hours talking. I was outside. Naked. Vulnerable. On my rooftop. Eavesdropping on two police officers parked below me. Their conversation was boring. If only they knew what fun they were missing above them. It was a long night not getting caught.

Late one night in the studio, we set fire to Sagittarius. She was a full-size sculpture of a woman in wire. She was stuffed full with dense branches of dried holly. We suspended her inside a double tetrahedron that spun from a rope twenty feet above us. We watched as Audrey set fire to the sculpture. It burned and spun in my studio late after midnight. The rope caught fire and flames climbed up into the rafters as she kept danced like a whirling Shiva. We were terrified and yet captured by the vision. The sculpture kept burning and spinning brighter and faster as the room filled with the whooping chants of spectators. None of us knew what would happen as the art was bigger than all of us. The destiny could have set this whole building on fire. As she spun her course, I saw the firelight reflected in the face of my muse. Audrey was a little girl again, watching her house burn down.

Brim opened his rucksack and pulled out five walkie-talkies. They were made of hard rubber and formerly colored a bright yellow. The yellow had been painted over with a black magic marker that had smeared off a few minutes later. Someone wrapped each one haphazardly in black duct tape. He seemed to read my mind looking at them. He jiggled the unit and said, "The black helps you stay Ninja." My chest began to fill with adrenaline. We were going into battle.

A guy was in the bathroom on his knees with the door open. He was leaning over the tub silk-screening a blood red fist on a black hoodie. I sat down at the kitchen table to inspect my walkie-talkie. I pretended it was an older model I hadn't seen before. My eyes peered concernedly as if I had found something peculiar. Then I decided it was all right after all. I was completely full of shit. But that didn't matter. I was in the hive of the fist.

I was a victim of a hit-and-run for about 45 minutes. She nailed me on my bicycle with a sporty white Honda. I rolled over her hood and made eye contact through the windshield. She looked concerned and checked the roadway to see if I still had my bicycle. She punched the gas and drove herself away in a flash. The tribal markings on her vehicle said she belonged to a gang of Greek women. Her escape route was up a hill where she could lose herself in campus traffic. I was bleeding, I was bewildered, and I was peddling as fast as I could after her. She dusted me easily up the hill but I kept climbing. I roamed the streets of that campus on squeaky brake pedals like a wounded mountain lion looking for an explanation. Howling with my eyeballs for my revenge. My chest was heaving in victimhood and I felt my jaw join forces with my neck. I dove into a thought experiment of finding her. What would I do except point at myself in grief. How would I heal in her sorry? I wanted was her acknowledgement but she already gave it. She told me it scared her when she hit me with her car so she drove away. I assume she never thinks about me. It would just scare her more and her mind would have to drive that much farther.

That was about the last time I was in Asheville. The city had turned itself into a city finally and I found it claustrophobic. I found a round house on top of a cold mountain in the highlands where skiers come to play in the snow. The seclusion was breathtaking and began my career as a hermit.

Gravity is Love

The earth loves us with her gravity. She pulls us back to her heart when we leap. She wants us to know what matters. Every morsel is important. Even the dust settles in her love. The sun loves the earth with its gravity. The earth loves the moon with hers. A child loves its mother from orbit. The secret force which we won't see, touch, or measure is love. Gravity is love.

CHAPTER EIGHT

Wizard of Oz

We witnessed the celebrity of the woolly worm. Its brown and black stripes predict the coming winter. An entire season of weekly snowfall foretold in the fur coat of an inchworm. People took them on stage to race them up strings. They announced the contestants, "Zippy," "Paul," and "Captain Speedy" over the microphone. Every worm was the crowd favorite. These slinky gladiators slaughtered the crowd with chuckles.

In the High Country, on this mellow lit Sunday, I saw corncob skyscrapers towering from the hands of children. Vendors pawned stories and knick knacks under temporary shelters. My senses were functioning flawlessly. The smiling war veterans, speckled with patches, commanded the festivities like karaoke at the Olympics. Nearby, tall boy scouts pawned soda cans for dollars. Flirty girls in denim clustered nearby pretending to be distracted. One girl in red watched the blue arms of a boy dive under the ice like a submarine.

After the day, we were pulled home by a tugboat of puppies. Down a hallway of forever's green, trimmed by a carpet of soil and stone, a sunset was just caught on camera. Music nudged our thoughts to the dance floor. We waltzed on dreams of new works to come as a show of fireflies and glossy stars opened its curtain. Back inside, beneath the shy flesh of a butternut squash, we found its orange perfection. We split her open down its middle, and brushed its lobes with butter. Tasting the gold flesh, I knew it was worthy of a poem.

I finally found her through 300 miles of copper wire and some help of directory assistance. Our first conversation in over a decade began like a job interview. She swam through every deep question like a trained dolphin. She spoke briefly of New York City, her writing, with a side of politics. My ears itched for the real sound of her voice below it. I wanted to ask her a question. I wanted her to ask me one. Anything. Instead, she said how great it was that we had done this. Her use of past tense fell on my foot like a bowling ball. The call had ended and I hadn't even started.

My courage phoned her again a few days later. Her telephone rang from the mudroom under some raincoats and galoshes. She pulled me out of her pocket and checked my name as she walked back in the kitchen. She placed me face down on the counter. She went back to installing the new dishwasher. My number fell into her call history like a trash compactor. My icon was twenty-four pixels tall, and just above a call from her dentist. Fifteen seconds later, her screen went dark to conserve battery.

On the other side of that phone, I was slouching. I had waited seven billion years to give her my virginity. All I wanted was a little forever. Was that too much to ask? Perhaps just a phone call every decade asking if she still remembers. When the fisherman casts his net too close to the rock of Gibraltar, he comes home at night hungrier than when he left.

It was a windy winter on Wizard Mountain as I jabbed myself through prickly trees to the Land of Oz. I found summit under a rusty chairlift drooping from its heartstrings. I stood atop a frozen emerald fountain and fought the roaring wind for its high ground. I found safety in a gazebo clinging to the cliff side. Behind the rail of this wind-torn confessional, I saw the eyes of the grandfather wizard gesturing me to tell. I expected some big question to spring forth from my lips. But I left my lack at home. I claimed my heart and mind to be fully seated. I spent my wish with a courageous silence. I mustered with the curled trees. We joined forces to tell the world the shape of the wind. We listened to the wizard's sermon together. His quartz white beard ran its wisp up to his temple. On a bridge of rocky eyebrows, so high you dare the valley to catch you, he spoke with thunder and lightning. He commanded the high country to click its heels three times. This was not a dream.

Snow's Trumpet

Can you hear the snow's quiet trumpet?
The silent song serenading the gray
Cold flakes falling in a ballroom of winter

As gravity tickles her gentle curtsy
Witness wet chastity dressed for her wedding
A feathery waltz down to soil's massive ache
Her frozen crystal in timeless perfection
How wickedly jealous the fire must be

I returned to running a year ago. I was building miles up and ready to try the Grandfather Marathon. I pictured the finish much like a woman might picture her prom night. My cummerbund matched the race course. My shoes were impeccable. It would be a clear moonlit night overlooking the city, with a plush down blanket and tons of stars. We would look deep into each other's eyes. Our naughty bits would tingle. Planets would align above love's perfection. Lionel Ritchie would write a song about it.

Then there is the reality of my marathon. The backseat of a sticky 1979 AMC Pacer with giant bulbous windows coated in steam. The sharp sun-crumbled vinyl seats mended with silver duct-tape. A long strip gets stuck to your sweaty butt-cheek as you try and say something romantic. Meanwhile, outside, a flickering streetlight showcases three alley-cats in heat. Their howling sirens joust in a dank and cloudy night against a dumpster. Humidity catches the bugs in mid-air as the syrup of fornication sticks to everything like wet candy.

The first part of my race was as easy, as the second part was difficult. Towards the end I had lost speech and hallucinated a purple alligator in a fedora. To be fair, he was very supportive of my condition. Around the final four miles an ambulance pulled up on the course alongside of me like a stalking mountain lion looking for an easy kill. He offered to take my carcass if I let him, but I insisted I could finish.

At the end of the race is a field on top of the mountain where men in kilts play bagpipes. It is the center of the Highland Games and my final lap of the marathon. The spectacle sets my heart on fire. It had already melted from the heat of me. My heart was melted and on fire and I was barely moving at all. I could feel the salt crystals grinding inside of each eyelash as I blinked. I probably would have covered more ground by walking. I was a plodding inchworm who just lost pole position to a butterfly on the second corner. I felt bad for anyone in the crowd hoping to behold a paragon. If only they knew that was me sprinting. I might have felt finished long before I finished but I finished. The mighty Orca ran a marathon.

My pack of panting lawyers know we are leaving before I do. They pulse by my side. They wag their intention. Arguments are wasted. They win every trial. These lawyers of panting demand my verdict. I will read from the transcript: "pant, pant, pant." None of this evidence can be contested.

The three of us roam as one. I fashioned a belt from two leashes with spring-action retraction. Every year replaced by their testament to adrenalin. Sometimes they pull so hard it bursts like a piñata. Bouncing springs and rolling gears die dramatically across the road.

They are my wagging metal detectors. They snooker every pocket of this mountain with their noses. With rear leg raised, they render a wet salute. Every sprout gets their blessing of holy urine. Give them time for their tongues must filter every windy molecule. Squirrels are warned. My pack will root you out like fury motored truffles.

Indian summer is the space in the bounce of a stone that's been skipped across the water. It creates an arc of anticipation. We find cherishment in mourning the loss of water's smooth face. It's a formal nod to the end of another warm season. It makes a perfect pocket to bask in the shine while fumbling with the idea of its passage.

As I come home, the tree's are booming in colors. As far as I can see, an army of brightness is marching up the mountainside. They charge the gentle blue sky with a cadence, "Winter is coming." They are personal, unique, and confident in their coloring prediction. If trees were blind, then God must truly lack compassion. These speckled soldiers need our voice to tell them they are beautiful. Let them turn our praise to vision. Let them feel our fingers caressing their trunk and absorb the whispers of lovers who thought they were alone. Promise me you will not speak for the trees. Instead, turn your head, and speak to them. Wrap yourself around their story like a torus. Listen to them say "thank you" for all your blessings.

Skin's Music

I feel your skin's music
I listen to it unfold
The rapture of its tiny electricity
You are a circuit to my battery
Your chest beats mine, every time

I beach myself in the tranquility of breathing
The soft wash of breath exhaled across my chest
I could win the world with the palm of your hand
Your body becomes my favorite song

It was a black tar bear of a September. My house sits almost at the top of a windy, cold mountain. Giant chunky boulders crest the dirt around me like giants. I was standing safe in my living room with my toes grounded in the carpet, looking at a fresh large Frasier fir outside my picture window. The tree was magnificent standing as high as my chimney. The branches seemed made of fresh frosting and jutted out from the trunk like perfect regal soldiers. As we breathed together, a feral tabby came barreling down from the ridge top. It launched itself into the bronchioles and sprang and climbed its way up the trunk. Before I had wonder, a huge avalanche of grunting and snorting came down in chase. A beastly ten-foot black tar bear grabbed hold of the evergreen throat and choked it over to break it. Like some Nephilim beanstalk, it stood fast and kept hold the refuge in its crow's nest.

The bear was heaving itself unsatisfied. His teeth were stained with menace. His fur sparkled with sweat as its muscles rippled under a rug of skin. His fists were impossible catchers mitts of rusted steel. He swatted them through the air like hot wet pirate cannons. The bear fell against the house as he scrambled for a better position on its dinner. My foundation was shaking from his addiction. Glass shattered as shelves toppled. Suddenly, the smell from my fearful breath seemed to catch its attention. It turned its giant cobra neck towards me and swelled as if it had gills. I was petrified in its searchlight. Its eyes were black, melting tar that oozed out of their sockets. It begets me its decision and barreled up my front steps as wood snapped and splintered underneath its thunder paws. The next thing I saw were the giant black fists clearing away my walls like the curtains. He was heaving as I rolled myself into a buttered crescent biscuit.

I heard a quick bark and landed on my bed in the fetal position. My dog was perched like a sphinx over top of me. His tail wagged concernedly. His head cocked a bit as he panted. He told me it was all right now. It was just a bad dream.

Why must I lust for my solitude? The court of public opinion had finally left the building. Minivans were packed full again and headed away. Trashcans jammed with confetti waited on the curbside. The snow was dumping as I shut the doors to my theater. There she was, my sweet solitude. The one who makes my toes breathe. She smirked from the back row as if she had been here this whole time. I know she dodged the fiasco. She knows in the madness of the season. A rising bog of mumbles creates a gas no one can escape. The same anecdotes play on the wall from obligation's projector. Pulsing beams broadcasting my manners on display for best in show. My attention is minced into snippets. Silence us slumped in the corner and slowly choking. Above his poor head I see sanity's chips falling like snowflakes from my ceiling.

But the madness is gone now. Nothing left but the sticky popcorn crunch under my feet. I smile back at my sweet solitude as we rekindle a quiet candle. I imagined her on the roof this whole time, tickling the stars with her gaze. She was always so good at disappearing over the company. And just like that she disappeared again as robotic footsteps broke through our moment. A lone spotlight lit the stage. Mr. Guilt stood in the center wearing a brown derby with matching vest. His back was straight. His arms bore a pile of spent costumes. A small metal strong box dangled from his pinky like a monkey. He cleared his throat and said, "I'll be leaving now."

Hey Life,

Do you hear that stomping? My giant was asleep for so many years you forgot his potential. I urge you make preparations. He is coming for you. One thing is certain. He is very hungry.

Life. I take from you this favor. When you cut me, make it deep and to the bone. From my blood drips a royal standard. It flaps high in the wind from a drumbeat deep and pounding. My will is an army thirsting to plunder. Let your strongest kings push me off this mountain. I want to claw my ugly way back to the top.

Life. Let your sun burn my face as they lounge under umbrellas. Watch me squirm and sweat as I swing my machete through your thick hot jungle. I will find your sacred artifact through the thickest pain and laughter. My pendulum swings far and heavy as it swaths through your world. And when you send death to fetch me, may he gulp at the proposition of taking me down.

A Better Man

Can a better man say no
Will he empty himself for affection

Shall he bend at every whim
Does he drive his own skin
A better man knows a lover like an engine
A better man follows his passion like a crow
A better man plants a seed in every season
A better man says nothing preferring only to show
Deep in the feet stands the better man
Tall in the spine gives him rest at night
He hunts the world from his neck like an eagle
He rules his mind like Kubla Khan

Her dreams were buried deep, below her proud standing. Here she was, in the high of day's noon. Sweat fell like raindrops from a broken gutter. The desert dust was keeping her eyes dry and clean. A space-aged shovel clanked on a boulder. It fell with the backpack she packed from home. Tools spilled loose from green army denim. She unwrapped a journal zipped safely in plastic. Pushing rubber buttons on the trusty gold Magellan, "Beep. Beep." came the assurance. This is where history would merge with the present. Kneepads shimmied their way over tied boots with effort. She had learned long ago the little things made the difference. She found the right spot in this dry dusty nowhere. Raising the shovel high like some temple queen, she plunged her spade deep into the earth. Bleeding rubble came spewing as she stabbed at her victim. She grunted in rhythm as the rocks crumbled cries of surrender. Hours passed gently. Her water was mental as she drank from the thought. Clank was the sound that would quench these lips open. She'd stop on the moment to bask in its time. By sunset she'd reach it, and pull loose her dirty clay bounty. The handle would squeak joyfully from attention. At that moment, she'd cross her legs and wipe her brow. Take a big drink. She'd be sure and cherish the reveal. Her hand brushed clean the container like a rescued box turtle. Deep inside, freed from the light of her shovel. Her secret would shine again.

Leslie had a wildlife sanctuary on the mountain. I started out as a volunteer one day when my dog found a feral kitten. Over the years I learned her trade of wildlife rescue. It was a dirty job, it was a dangerous job and it came without a salary. I became a wildlife wrangler and education coordinator. I took animals to schools and gave presentations. I found great satisfaction in my job with no pay and eventually became their president.

He was a great-horned owl. When I first met him he was meaner than a snake on absinth. He hated me and us and the habitat and the surgery that took part of his wing off. He hated that barbed wire fence that stopped him from catching that rabbit. I was bribing him with mouse guts. He would pulse his throat feathers on high speed and twist his neck around like a possessed girl when I entered. He wanted to rip my face off. I knew then we would be best friends. Many mice later, I summoned the courage to snatch his beak like a game of got-your-nose. I shook it like a handshake and said, "Nice to meet you." I held him there and stuck my eye in front of his eye and told him, "We are friends now." It was scary but he was on the glove in two more weeks.

I found three foxes. I hated how it happened. Each day I set a trap of peanut butter for the next one. They were all babies in their burrow. They were forced into my trap by hunger. They did not know I had buried their mother. It took five days to capture all three of them. Each day they huddled in their abandoned dirt corner. They kept losing each other one-by-one. The fourth would never come out. I never saw him but I feel certain there was another. I stuck my arm in the hole as far as it would go. I was reaching for its trust. The orphan had no concept of the hand of mercy. Back in my bathroom, three red orphans are crying behind a porcelain tree trunk. My cat sprays the outside of the door to show us all his feelings. I am a fox foster for eleven weeks. We build them a habitat and they grow from free bacon and cantaloupe. We have to watch them by camera. Benevolence knows to stay out of the picture. They are big and strong now. I left the door open with food but they stopped coming. They are finally foxes again.

Last night my head leaped out from a car window. The wind inflated my cheeks like a parachute. My eyeballs turned sticky from the chill in the air. My belly was fizzing with romantic bubbly. We were two people, traveling just below the canopy of southern Appalachia. I was already home, squinting at the thought of us in the distance. Here, on our carriage of four cylinders, secretly wishing we could drive forever.

Events start and stop. Pleasure spreads ripples through our memories. Dr. Simon and Mr. Garfunkel lend us their tune. The best parts are when you are singing. The harmony of all this sound double-bounces my heart right out of my throat. My lips erupt their precious secret, "let's keep falling higher and higher. Life's balloon gave me this one string. And the levity of you pulls my whole world up, up and away."

How vivid was the confidence that brought you up this mountain. So high we stand together, faces cradled in the wind. There is no fear to keep your wondrous eyes from peeking. Vaulted more by a simple press of tiptoe on the edge. A giant valley of doubt crumpled far below us. We come from that bottom. We were baptized in her river. Time-and-again, our squishy boots have squeaked their way home. For years the spine rested in the shape of a question. Now with nerves untwisted, we form a proud exclamation. Here, drink love's water, from my roots to your branches. Under our tree, we cast this blanket. We nibble on the fancy fruit of our labor. Together, up here, among the raptors.

When Knees Touch Ground

When knees touch ground
the sacred seem to listen
Knees rarely bend in trivia
Like a page folded from our story
Knees mark a wrinkle on a silky road
A ridge worth a peak from heaven
We kneel for God to listen
We bend to prove our quiet

Knees ground when we fail
They sink when we weep
They fold when we fall
They burrow when we surrender
But all is not lost when our knees fall
On our knees we plant a seed
From our knees we learn to crawl
And on a knee we promise forever

The teeth of the saw were mincing through the limb like a corncob. Shrapnel chips fell like a blizzard all over our shoulders until the roof was free of its intruder. The air was hot as we hovered over the severed bicep of a fallen southern oak. The flesh was still steaming from the trauma. As wood bled its hot glue in the driveway, he held his chainsaw on a pole like it was a long spear. We chitchatted over the carcass as the night rose.

I kept the pin in my grenade I was about the drop. The waiting was painful. Small talk takes even longer when you want the right moment. Finally, a space broke in the river and I leaned out into the current. I asked the man with a chainsaw for the blessing of his daughter. I won't tell you what I told him. The promise I gave him. It makes it more sacred this way. Men are born to give words to each other privately. The privacy makes them a covenant. We sealed our vocal pact with a handshake. Each would sleep alone that night with the new guarded secret of the men's club.

She played canasta in the kitchen with her mother. They sat across from each other like they were in a mirror. I saw where one face was going. I saw where another face had come from. The table was a merry-go-round of every topic but the one. The men of the house were playing games with their ladies.

In the closet, under the stairs, in the fridge, on the shelf, in the drawer, was a shiny-waxed box. In the box was a yellow cake dressed in white frosting and decorated with pastel flowers. Under that frosting he was the saddest cake there ever was. He hummed the saddest song muffled under a frosty blanket. He was locked in his box, tucked in its drawer, high on its shelf, deep in the fridge, behind the sealed door, in the closet, under the stairs, and in the house. No one could tell how sad he was.

The next day, someone came into the closet and opened the fridge, slipped open the drawer, pulled out the box from the shelf. They opened the box and pulled out the cake hiding under its frosting. They stabbed it with candles and set fire to the tips. The candles dripped wax on the frosting while voices sang in joy and the cake was cut. It was split down the middle and columned and rowed. After it's body was chopped and put on plates and carried out to tables under a bright sun. Forks were jabbed into each of its parts. Teeth sunk deep into the yellow flesh that once sang. Tongues rolled and mushed the cake into tiny balls that rolled down the throats and into dark little bellies of boys and girls. Deep in the dark, the yellow cake was happy again and sang a beautiful song about sugar.

A woman from Asheville did a reading on me once. She told me all about my future while I sat and listened politely. I should have listened better. She spoke of a cold, cold mountain and a wolf howling on the summit. She said this to me when I lived in the valley. She had to have seen this coming. We took two wolves from someone who should not have had them. We did our best to find them something better. We laid electric fence around an enclosure with a shelter. We tossed them deer parts over the high fence walls. They ate in giant gulps and chomps. They tore bone clean apart. I could hear their howls from home six miles away. I told my town they would stop for no one or nothing. They were our wild toothy violence behind an electric fence. I had to go in there for sanitation. I sat down on the ground outside their entry most nights and ate my dinner. I would throw them scraps of rotisserie to draw them close to me. I was showing them my prowess at flavor. I licked my fingers exaggeratedly in front of their faces and showed them my growling teeth. I would urinate in front of the entrance as much as possible. I was deadly serious about this being was my front gate.

Carnivore

Gather around me all blessed creatures
I come to eat of you up one after one
My eyes are the forks I use to pluck you
My ears slit your throat to drink from your lung
Your juice is my gravy that rolls down my gullet
My teeth are stained from your bloody release
Your bones beat the trophy I made of your skin

I suckle the cobalt that winks from your mane
I bite in the crackle the creaks from your beak
I gnaw on each hoof and lick clean the neck
I am your beholder your carnivore king

It was a wildcat so I put on a catchers mask. I put on welding chaps made for the arms and shoulders. My neck was wrapped in a thick pink towel. I wore leather raptor gloves. I was climbing into a cage with a live bobcat. This was not a metaphor. We were going to stick a needle in its mane to transport it. All I had to do was push it up against the side of the cage so Leslie could give the injection. She locked me in the antechamber. It was too short to stand up so I was crouching. I looked at her one-last time and she asked me if I was sure I wanted to do this. I was sure I wanted to do this.

I entered the wildcat's octagon. The habitat was about as big as a parking space. The bobcat was fearful and pacing. I asked Leslie if I should just grab it. She said that wouldn't be necessary. She was right. He was swinging his back hips like whiplash on a roller coaster. He was metaphorically cracking his knuckles and folding his neck from side-to-side. He was sizing me up and knew I was scared. He thought my outfit was ridiculous. He calculated my weak spot and struck like a sledgehammer at my torso. His muscles made him as heavy as an eighty-pound bag of concrete. He was made from solid, flexible granite. He had come to pull my neck out and my forearms were the only things stopping him. His front claws were curling around my wrists like a boa constrictor. I felt intelligence in his murder. He was trying to pry me open with my bones as his lever. He was pumping his back claws into my torso with quick short strokes. He was a velociraptor cutting a cow's guts out. My adrenaline ignited. I wore him like a double-armed shield as I forced him into the corner. Both our lives were fragile and we shared in a moment of desperation. My eyes watched his slowly fall under the tranquilizer. In seven minutes I went from fighting him off like a devil to carrying his sweet delicate body like a baby. His urine was noxious and powerful. His coat hair was thick as whiskers and sharp as cactus. I rocked a demon baby's sleeping body in my arms till we got him home.

Ten years prior, I spent a night in the woods with two juveniles who had been behaving badly. As their counselor, my job took them out deeper into the woods, away from main camp, into a more primitive setting of survival. We ate meals out of cans and generally waited for the therapy of survival to do something positive. Our second night out we heard the cry of the wildcat. If you've never heard its call, it sounds like a hovering demon baby with its body on fire. The shrieking terror in its call will change you forever. It was thirty yards away at our compost pit. It circled the camp and smoked us out with its terror ritual. The kids thought I was pretending not to know what the sound was. I could not say it was a hovering demon baby whose body was on fire. That bobcat was a better counselor than I was.

I am running for town council in my tiny ski town of three hundred people. I am sitting behind a table in our community center. There is a white crisp tablecloth hiding my shoes and someone has made everyone coffee in the corner. What used to be the yoga room is now full of chairs with a person in each one of them. The whole town is here and I'm not sure what I have gotten myself into. Small town politics had grown hysterical lately and I suppose I heard the call to preach. I watch a retired woman grill each of the candidates about our town's deer problem. She is a part-timer with another home in the city of Charlotte. She wants the deer gone and complains, "They have their babies under our deck." She thinks the town should do something about these crack addicts with hooves. I am one of six candidates and seated last in order. I am what you would call the fringe candidate. The wild card. I take my roles very seriously.

The three incumbents inform the lady how hard they've been working on her problem. They quote studies from state wildlife officials about deer tick and lice as they each make a case about how sensitive they are to her issue. The next two candidates suggest the incumbents have not been sensitive enough and convince her they would bring a higher level of sensitivity. Most of them were discussing euthanasia.

When it was finally my turn, I asked the lady if there was a deer problem in Charlotte. She told me succinctly there was not one. I asked if she had considered staying in Charlotte for the entire year. You could tell by her answer that she had never considered my idea before. She seemed to almost feel insulted by it. Some people thought I was joking when I then pressed the idea we should consider giving our deer the right to vote. In the back of my mind, I had developed this maverick political stance as some sort of deer Lorax. I was convinced this strategy was brilliant.

Like a lot of my running, I came in last. I believe eleven votes were cast in my favor. Not one of them came from a deer. Had they, I'm sure I would have won in a landslide.

I have not started this pen in a long time. Vroom. Vroom. I sputter meaningless gravel of letters. I cough from the metaphorical diesel smoke. I lay down a few curses. So much choke it croaked. Let's wait a sentence. Is there a rumble in this pen? Try again. Not again. I hold my mouth right and re-squeeze the trigger. Go figure. Nothing but fragment. I place my gaze inside the chrome mirror wired to the end of the handlebar. I stomp into her pedal deeply. It cranks and then tanks. A leaky preposition. This cycle will change. Strange. Fragment. Think. These words are too weak to seat. Does my love ride sissy or sidecar? My throne of bone is so alone. My attempts to rectify are gaping lizards. I am a lime green spider on a bridge of silk, trying to catch a Volkswagen Beetle. I'd find it easier to strangle water with my fingers. Or tie this rope around the wind. Steal me please a brittle piece to consider. With my mouth full of taffy, I can piddle and fiddle while we comb the gum out of hope's beard. Stay with me. Through spark and wrench we trip to drip. I am fingering oil along the moist seal of a round rubber gasket. Clapping my hands off on the sides of these bibs. A motor is a metallic chunk of failure delayed by a good mechanic. Ok, friend. Try again. Turn the grip. Let 'er rip. Vroom. Vroom.

Tulips Kiss

In the dawn I lay to kiss this tulip.

I admit we've flirted now for days.
Its face is cloistered in a tall green spire.
I could not guess her true colors underneath.
On my knees, my two lips to this tulip.
My two lips wet her bud of folding fingers.
A Woodpecker pounded its gavel for decency.
Our garden converted to a nunnery.
I decide to rise and practice my saunter.
Catching sun's first ray with my merry men.
Two dogs, and a dwindling cat,
in the garden of pious tulips.

James' skin was blacker than soot and stretched like a limo across a tight frame of muscle. He lived underneath my beach hut in Placencia. The carpet in his home was pure beach sand but it had four walls and a ceiling. He owned three possessions for his occupation: a cinderblock, fishing tackle, and a cell phone. He would hide the cinderblock in case someone tried to steal it. One night he hung it in from a tree. Sometimes he took the time to bury it. The block was important to him. He used it for strewn fishing lines that stumbled into the surf like the tracks of turtles. He was a primitive and gifted hunter.

I found him on the beach alone late at night motioning me over. He was on a phone call and he wanted me to sit down to listen. I sat next to him and pressed my head against his so I could hear a lady speaking through the speaker. The wind made it difficult so we burrowed our skulls closer to form a cavern. I felt his cheeks smile as she was talking. He was motioning with his fingers as if showing me the words as they went by. She told James how much she loved him and that she was divorcing her husband. James was showcasing his prowess for me. He wanted someone to bear him witness. He was reeling in a forty-year-old woman like a grouper.

James told me the days when he was called "Black Pharaoh." He roamed the streets of Belize City as king of the block. He brandished a gold-plated gun that gleamed against a shiny matching Cadillac. He would parade the streets in black muscular skin adorned only with gold and jeans. He never spoke of his exile from the city. One sunset I watched his silhouette straddling the sides of a row boat in the harbor. He was the Pharaoh trawling for more bait.

I am diving. I cross my arms like a pharaoh and fall backwards from the weight of my tanks of a boat. The salt water surrenders itself kindly to my body. I am finally sinking on purpose. I see a large remora suckerfish through the blue across the water. She is idling across a long stretch of ocean. I check my oxygen and clear a schedule for recess. I reach out and call her with my telepathy. I imagined myself a successful and generous turtle. I send her a mental invitation of mouth scraps for the taking. I lurch my back sideways in play and swim in a slow spiral. I send sonar from my forehead as I wait for an answer. I finally forgive her for not responding, and turn my turtle body and flipper home. I can track my party's bubbles hopscotching back to the surface. My swim is jolted as my chest is boarded by the suction slits of remora. My little tiny shark torpedo took a table for one with an ocean view. I try not to act so surprised or excited. I am a teenager pretending he's kissed lots of girls before. Remora's elegant body is as long as my torso. I give her slippery silver a stroke before folding my hands behind my back like wings. I focus on the grace of my pump and breathing. I am a fin-powered tour bus with a passenger from the terminal who thinks she parked under the tube coral in Lot C. We draw lazy circles together up and down the reef. Remora and me had fun as one, eighty feet below the surface of Belize.

Sea Pines

My crannies gurgle in your jetsam
You fill in all my deep places
Willets jab deep and tenderize my skin
Your silky cloak spills over-and-over
A slippery dolphin rides you home
I am your one true shore
Crash into me
Surrender your foam and bubble
The sun bleeds marmalade forever
My fingers ride your soapy skin
Your cheeks soaked in my lips
We are sand and water

CHAPTER NINE

Six Dragons

I married a dragon in skin. She had a mane and a tail and was fond of me once. I took her to Belize and she expressed our pleasure in her nakedness. Her nipples peeked behind two hands caressing a punctured coconut. I remember how lucky that straw was giving juice to her lips. I felt her eyes shoot fire into mine. I had never been so deeply in love again.

She dosed me with dopamine like a pin prick from a tiny scorpion. She blew colored smoke that tickled my childhood. She carried torches for every one of my dreams and worshipped my stature on a pedestal. She told me I unlocked her gnosis as she hailed me as a kingpin. She wrapped her sweet thighs around my trunk and called me her sequoia. She played my strings like a maestro and made all of it seem so real. The smoke was so colorfully kind back then from the mouth of dragonus narcissus.

my sweet passion's fruit
her life's juice drips orgasm
on my teeth and lips

Her father was a retired executive. I watched him struggle with his memory. He was looking at pictures constantly on a computer trying to remember the faces. They called it a sideshow. I knew he was not reminiscing. When I became his son-in-law, he became a father. I took this role very seriously. I watched a man lose a battle with his mind alone in front of his family. Once, I candidly rescued him from a fall in the bathroom. He was always alone. They just thought he liked photography.

Oh memory's tower, how long overdue is this inspection. Today, I behold thee, my monument to passing. You are my stronghold, my bastion of definition. Without your shelter I fade into oblivion. You turn taller with each day lived fully. Overlooking a forgetful sea, you stab through night's curtain as my beacon of meaning. Your every stone is a story, and each crack a tear. Today, I find your foundation lacking. I see empty spaces once filled with something that's gone now. Who takes your stones away? Where are these cursed vandals hiding? So busy are we in our stacking, day-upon-day. I never imagined you would grow so tall, nor crumble so freely.

From this height I can survey all my intentions. A seasoned life may be too salty for brick. How long will you stand up in this pounding? How far will you shine for me into the darkness? You are my rock, my anchor, and my tall, proud captain. I salute thee. How blessed to know you. How thankful to not forget.

She decided it was over about ten weeks after our wedding. She did not feel her decision was any of my business. Months later, I watched her peel me from the surface of her eyeballs like a contact lens. She took my six millimeter tall body and placed it on the shelf with the rest of the plastic people. She ended the negotiation in less than thirty minutes. Our very last night together she fought me over a power cord. She decided she wanted to keep it. I told her "no" so she grabbed me by the scrotum and twisted. She wrapped her fingers around the cord like a rope swing. She was gnawing at it like an animal. She would come over the next day and show me she was sorry. She would show me the beautiful pretty smoke. She liked to play with me like that.

Dragonus Narcissus

I am trapped in your triangle. My kind words bounce off your elegant skin. Affections dissolve over the boiling heat from your furnace. You are dangerous and I am cobblestone. Dig in your heels if that's all I get. I have been locked inside this craving for your touch. Your touch is something. And something is so much less now than it used to be.

I tried to draw your mad squiggly line. Now I walk it like a tightrope stretched between loyal and foolish. I made you six dragons because I missed those steep fangs. I missed the silky arson of your lips. I lay lamenting the times they tasted like candy. Back when you believed in me.

So many sunsets, just me and your voicemail. You are my charming dragon. Your grace is reptilian. Your teeth are perfect. Your eyes are deadly. Cast me a spell from your glittering tongue. You will always be so very pretty.

My first bamboo dragon was my last attempt to save a marriage. I wanted her to see beauty come out of the man she said was worthless. I thought the juxtaposition would shatter the prison for both of us. But I was in a triangle again, this time with a little girl and her reptile. I wanted my wife back. I thought I could make plasma in my hands like Annie did for me. My plasma backfired and I found myself caught in a pit of codependency. It cracked me wide open and I just kept breaking over-and-over.

I pushed my wife. Back. I pushed her, back. She had pushed me against a metal door chime that went square into my back. I pushed her back. That was wrong and I owned it. I still do; I pushed her. I have no skill at taking pushes. When she saw how sorry I was, there was a distinct pause in her thinking. Something clicked for her but she would not share it. It would be a surprise.

I showed up precisely on time in a business park pushed into a green hillside. I pushed into a chair in front of a communal hot water kettle with a dim red light on. I watched it burn while a group of clinical psychologists mingled behind a cracked door. They were listening for the front door to open. I was the only one who had no idea what was coming. When she pulled up, three women and a man rushed out and pushed her past me like paparazzi. They took the starlet behind the door and pushed it closed. It opened again long enough for one of them to say they'd be with me shortly. It was a long time. I thought we were meeting a new marriage counselor. I was about to discover her surprise.

When I came in, someone began to speak for her. I burst into tears just from seeing her face. They were speaking for her so she didn't have to. I assumed they would hear me after so I nodded empathically and listened to them tell me her story. I accepted each accusation as my craving for everyone's opinion grew stronger. I remember thinking we would have a breakthrough because of their witness. We could come clean here. I kept expecting my turn to come but it kept not coming. If only I had pushed it.

The older man and woman took her out of the room. I was left with two younger women still in college. One of them asked if she could tell me a story. I started laughing on top of crying, and I shook my head, no. My answer did not matter. She wanted me to hold a crayon and draw my feelings on the paper. She looked at me with pathetic condescension. She was proud of her newfound monster and she wanted to poke it to see if it was breathing. Since I would not take her quill, she did it for me. She drew methodical rings on a sheet of paper with a maroon crayon like a circling buzzard. She decorated me with her costume and told me about my endless cycles of evil. She said I could break the chain by declaring myself toxic.

I asked her when it was my turn but she deflected my question. She said, let's focus on you now as we ignored me together. I had been summoned here to sign a confession in crayon. I was so low then I believed them. For the next year, I paid the same business park every week to tell me about my danger. A man would watch my gestures with an exaggerated look as if my hands were on fire. He would give me a quiz with his mobile phone asking me to push a dot across the screen so he could know what kind of job he was doing. He could have asked me but he trusted the dot more.

At a place called Spirit Lake in Florida near the Suwannee, the short girl called me a wife beater. Then she said, "You're not welcome here." She told me I could not camp anywhere nearby with a broad swooping arm gesture. I remember her toast to me in front of a fire last fall. She didn't know me then either but she told everyone how great I was. I was no longer one of her tribe. The fakest one pretended to give me a hug. It felt like dissonance and his smile was all teeth. I realized it didn't matter what really happened. His allegiance was to my wife, not the truth. They all were this way and it took so little to turn them. I don't remember trying to argue with them. My chest felt like a jar of June bugs buzzing my new nickname. I had never been called a "wife beater." I just stood there stunned in the trauma. A tribe of flying monkeys in Florida put a spell of words in my chest while I stood there. That was the first day of my first dragon and I built it alone. The same short girl would walk by and tell me, "Good job, wife beater!" It made them feel good to say it loudly. That night, in the dark, I drove far away from everyone and camped in a field near a fence under the cold pulsing stars. It was freezing and the sky kept winking her eyes at me saying, "We know the truth." It felt beautiful under her reassurance. I woke up in the sunrise covered in dew. I sat up in the truck bed and found a flock of emu next to me eating breakfast. I felt ostracized last night and I seemed to know where my home was. The next night, one of the other artists handed me his apple and a lighter. I took a bite out of it and noticed it tasted like fresh marijuana. Apparently I had just swallowed his organic smoking apparatus. I became one of their friends after everyone stopped laughing. They were beautiful people and gave me hope I would again find a tribe.

Word of my new nickname spread from Florida to Ohio. Friends from the road became a source of constant wondering if maybe their silence meant something different. I was constantly riding shotgun with my own paranoia. I discovered there was no honor among men. She marked a friend of mine with her sex a few months later showing me the entrance to her territory. He fell as easily for her as I did. Her smoke is blown for others now. I have never felt so sad, burned and discarded. I didn't know it at the time but her dragon knows I am perceptive. It fears me. It did everything it could to destroy me and it worked. The whole experience murdered who I was. It would be a year more of depression before I'd even want to come back. I remember buying a lottery ticket one morning just to give me something to look forward to. It was money well spent but it showed me how far I had crashed. Dragon narcissus doesn't want you to lay down and die, it wants you to lay down and bleed.

There you pine, jailed in that rib cage. The little plastic army men keeping you at bay. Turnstiles click at each year's passing. Neon slashes of chalk marking each day. Three meals a day, fingers grasp the tray of flimsy brushed metal compartments in division. Filled with the same ladle of different gruel. There is creamed corn. Sweet potato. And cherries jubilee. The warden's face is very familiar. Dare you put your finger on the name? You are soaking in your own pitiful hot springs. You are a shiny cipher, hiding your own solution. A dangling wind chime, stuffed mute with cotton. A picture window scratched deep by an angry diamond. Lounging on your own hands as you sit on a porch swing. Watching the hungry wolves tend your sheep.

My next commission was called the Mothership and required me renting an old gas station. We built her out of plywood in the three-bay garage with a crew. The craft was a ginormous tripod with knees and ankles. We painted it rusty red and her top was foam and wood. She stood sixteen feet high and each joint was fully adjustable. Her legs were so big they spilled out of the bay doors. The spectacle stopped traffic like the stone lion. People wanted to know what we were doing. I was trying to fly as far away as I could.

The Mothership was a very identifiable non-flying object. It had nearly a thousand lights and sixteen remote controls. Each foot spat out fog between its lit toes and made the ground look like a space port. I had made my own machine of fancy colored smoke. The Mothership debuted at a Wisconsin festival as a wild Indian jumped with his guitar off a plank wailing a song about freedom.

My Mothership attracted a new woman. My hot iron dipped in her water and sizzled in the chemistry. She tried to seduce me with a story of the velveteen rabbit. I knew then that she was like the last one. She wanted to tickle my childhood. I can smell these reptiles now. I could smell the dragon through her cuffed shorts as my hand hiked her thigh up on the stove. I am addicted to this potion and madly in love with dragon narcissus.

Swan

How soft did she bloom from the chest?
My senses sip her possibility
The neck of a swan held communion in shoulders
Worry perching on the curve of a brow
The fidelity of softness dilates my pores
Looking so steeply down a gently bridged nose
I watch the sun as it crests in her honey
Her amber yolk of longing in a crisp white virgin
The radiation cracks open this lake
Paddle away on a petticoat of ripples
Au revoir my sweet silky thing

They invited me to build my third dragon at Electric Forest. The mighty trees of the Sherwood Forest fawned over acres of colorful art buildings and sculpture. Our team mounted and coiled a flexible irrigation pipe around a cluster of trees. We cut bamboo into thousands of dragon scales and screwed every one of them to the pipe from ladders. We decorated the head with thick green moss and gave her a lush red tongue of rose pedals. We suspended the head between two trees from wire so the wind could dance it in the breeze. The dragon stared you right between the eyes from an observation balcony. Sherwood Forest was surrounded by clans of artists working together and I was one of them.

That night I heard the sound of DJ Bass Nectar. After the show I got caught up in a sea of leftover zombies. They were young and spun like dizzy bees and bouncing off each other with nowhere to go. They had suckled his giant speakers but the sound was gone and they were lost and hungry. I could have led them over a cliff with a drum. I knew what it looked like to be lost. I came upon a woman touching my dragon with reverence. She breathed in every scale and stroked its every hump. She told me her sad story as I sat next to her and listened. She hugged me and said thank you. I was proud to see my dragon working.

Under the festival moonlight I walked back to my tent with a tall staff of bamboo. I noticed my long shadow stretched way out ahead of me while I was marching. Inside of my flowing fleece poncho, a wide brimmed hat, and a staff with a long streamers, I could see the shadow of my wizard. He was so tall and confident now. I was riding atop my pelvis mesmerized by this identity. Just then a young woman screamed in fright as I passed her. She told me I was terrifying and I offered nothing to console her. I held none of the responsibility. I had lost my codependence and was resonating from my own heart beat now.

Embrace your burning ashes. Fall hard every single time. Crash and smash into the rocks. Become a messy smoking heap. In the stillness of your death, watch and listen. You will hear the drum beats of your rebirth. Your spine is a mighty resilient antenna. Tune in to your frequency. Hear their message from the stars. Their dust is your clay. All life begins in a supernova.

They wanted a dragon in Costa Rica. I flew down with nothing but an electric hand drill. The mornings grew so hot I took siestas in town among the watermelon. I am slurping one now as slowly as possible. I have been electrocuted by the sky's big yellow bug light. A local woman behind the bus counter is exorcising me with her eyelashes. She's hung a flyer in Spanish warning everyone about the visiting dirty gringos. She makes it clear I am one of them. I don't speak her language but she is slapping the sign and pounding her own chest at me in anger. She is forced to sell me a ticket. She keeps shaking her head back-and-forth and scolding me in Spanish. I can see how torn she is by the transaction. She wants me gone but doesn't want to touch my money. Her anger bounced off my chest like a breast plate.

I awoke from my tent to the sound of howler monkeys calling me lazy. I spend the morning taking bamboo with my team in the jungle. We drag the slaughtered tube carcasses back to our circle. We are building a giant basilisk lizard three stories high overlooking the jungle. For lunch I bond with strangers as renegade chickens too quick for last night's axe peck at buried treasure. At sunset, we all salute each other down on the beach in a gathering. Just like the monkeys, a human howling breaks out every evening as the sun goes down. I can never tell which one of them starts it.

A man named Hayes hides behind a fold-out table guarded by rows of stacked clipboards. Because he spins records he doesn't think he should have to be here. He makes people wait in the sanctity of his opinion. There are dozens of volunteers fresh off the bus wanting to help us build a jungle party. We are one big gypsy pirate family. He pretends to be too busy for them as he struts in front and lectures about things they have not done. He scolds a young couple for standing too close to his personal space as he pantomimes how big he sees himself. With zero forethought, I stepped up to the front and scold him squarely in public. I remind him we were in the jungle. I made everyone silent except me. I was firm and I saw his energy clearly. He was evacuating the enthusiasm of fresh faces and sucking energy through his nostrils like smoke. He was stunned by my truth. I placed my machete on a shoulder and dragged my decapitated bamboo away and left him.

On the way back to the states, I shared a cab with a retired couple and a chubby fellow who had just landed. He was telling the couple about his new bride to be. He was on his way to pick her up from some foreign country. He told us how their relationship was special; how it was a very deep and spiritual connection. I couldn't tell if I had more envy or pity to give him. I gave him neither. I was just here for the lizard.

God vs Man

The creature of man shat out its tail while walking
His lizard inside grew it back to do him a favor
His mind took note and cut it off with a hatchet
This cycle repeated, over-and-round again

Finally God asked man what he was doing
Man said he didn't want it anymore
God was sad because he spent a long time on it

CHAPTER TEN

A Great Awakening

A new infantry has mustered here on this cold foggy morning. They come to spill blood over your brain's gentle creases. Two forces fighting for control of the rebel inside you.

These armies of infantry want to tame your creature with the whips of shame and the fruits of fame. One side will praise it for its splendor and relish its coating. They will fatten its ears with fatty lies and words of perfume. The other will trap and brand your beast with the marks of sinner or bigot. It will convince your wretch it is broken. They will tell you it cannot be trusted. And you nodded in agreement a very long time ago. You tied its neck for them as they slipped the cold metal bar in its bite. And we are born to believe these masters are magnanimous. We believe we are at our best when humble and cooperative.

But we said goodbye to the beast inside. That beautiful sasquatch of hair and emotion is howling to the sky and he has never needed a reason. He's calling you back to his forest moon. For many, life seems tasty behind the safety of glass. We remain subdued and coddled by the armies that infiltrate our reason. So many noble soldiers chained by what they have been taught was loyalty. They are starving for a chance to be wrong so they may choose another side. This chained inner voice is a revolution in waiting.

Maybe you have found yourself recruited to one of these armies. Maybe you've caught yourself sabotaging your own side a few times. You've kept things introspective while you process your feelings. One night, while stirring, you reach under your pillow for a cool place to park your fingers. You bump a book inscribed "A Manifesto" in your handwriting. The author's name is your own. But you do not remember. Your heart is beating so much faster. You smuggle this contraband to the bathroom away from your platoon. Camouflaged in the stall, with your pants rolled around your ankles. You quietly crack open this sacred tomb and begin to awaken. These words turn gears inside you. You find a secret psychic compartment with a message. You discover yourself to be a spy in your very own mind.

You embrace your own story. Deep in your essence was a sleeping prisoner. A Clockwork Orange Rambo was strapped to a barber chair for decades. Eyelids were gagged open by cold stainless pinchers as visions of wild horses were broken and branded all with the pounding cones of giant speakers that kept repeating, "You are broken." Again and again. "You are broken." Year after year. "You are broken!" But somehow, your orangey mutant freak unhinged itself from the armchair and crawled you out of the cave.

And here you are panting like a fugitive from prison. You are atrophy and hunger. The raw truth of the sun is a blinding hot fire. You feel the shivery withdrawals of societal obligation. You are flying cold turkey. Your gut has revolted from the chants of "I can't be trusted." You hear your friends and family calling you back with "Have a seat," and "Take it easy." You remember how the system uses faith and loyalty to keep you there. Are you a good boy? I wait for your answer. I said louder, are you a good boy?

I did not think so.

You have just killed your master. In his blood you introduce yourself to its new reflection. You are Rōnin in the empire of your mind. Your life is a fresh papyrus bearing the calligraphy of each decision. Each character from your brush is the ink-blood of your freedom. You are the source of your own definition. And as your prophecy predicted; when the world spilt its light upon from heaven, your soul rose up to feel it outside of the cave.

SKETCHES

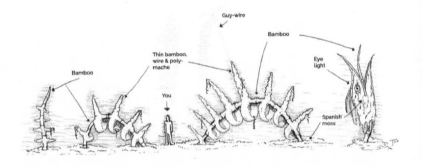

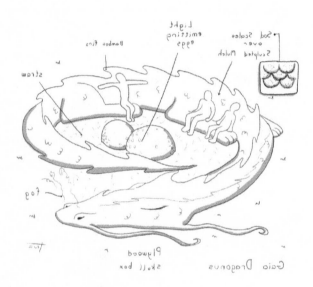

Light
emitting
eggs

Bamboo fins

Straw

Sod Scales
over
Sculpted Mulch

fog

Plywood
Skull box

Gaia Dragonus

106

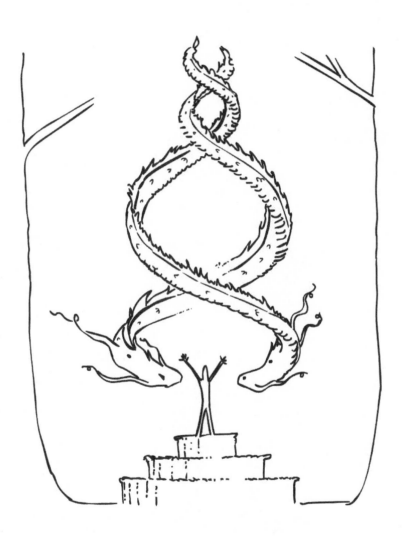